iPractice

Essential Music Technology: The Prestissimo Series
Richard McCready, *Series Editor*

Digital Organization Tips for Music Teachers
Robby Burns

Recording Tips for Music Teachers
A Practical Guide for Recording School Groups
Ronald E. Kearns

iPractice
Technology in the 21st Century Music Practice Room
Jennifer Mishra and Barbara Fast

iPractice

Technology in the 21st Century Music Practice Room

Jennifer Mishra

AND

Barbara Fast

Oxford University Press is a department of the University of Oxford. It furthers the University's objective of excellence in research, scholarship, and education by publishing worldwide. Oxford is a registered trade mark of Oxford University Press in the UK and certain other countries.

Published in the United States of America by Oxford University Press
198 Madison Avenue, New York, NY 10016, United States of America.

Library of Congress Cataloging-in-Publication Data
Names: Mishra, Jennifer, author. | Fast, Barbara (Pianist), author.
Title: iPractice : technology in the 21st century music practice room / Jennifer Mishra, Barbara Fast.
Description: New York : Oxford University Press, 2019. | Includes index.
Identifiers: LCCN 2018005876 (print) | LCCN 2018008291 (ebook) | ISBN 9780190660918 (updf) |
ISBN 9780190660925 (epub) | ISBN 9780190660901 (alk. paper) | ISBN 9780190660895 (alk. paper)
Subjects: LCSH: Music—Instruction and study—Technological innovations. | Practicing (Music)
Classification: LCC MT1 (ebook) | LCC MT1 .S65 2918 (print) | DDC 780.7/7—dc23
LC record available at https://lccn.loc.gov/2018005876

Contents

Preface

This whole project started with Measure 66.

It was Christmas. I was working on a premiere with Spectrum Trio, *Litanies*, by Marilyn Shrude, and found myself struggling with one particular melismatic passage in a handwritten score. Measure 66. I tried writing in the notes, different fingerings, uneven rhythm practice, all to no avail.

My brother, Arlen Fast, was also in the middle of working on premiere works, almost one a week, with the New York Philharmonic. Via email and phone calls I had been hearing about his various practice technics, usually involving his laptop, to learn new music—quickly.

In the midst of a long vacation, both practicing in separate rooms, I shared a proverbial musicians frustration: *I just don't seem to be getting any better with this passage!* In reality, it was one measure. How hard can it be?

"Let me see if I can help you," was Arlen's response, and he pulled out his laptop.

And proceeded step-by-step to input the notation of measure 66, into his computer, first adding 8va's to any extreme ledger lines.

Voilà! Magical. I instantly could almost sight read the measure.

The next step was to add in bar lines. What meter might work? All of a sudden the seemingly random notes felt even easier to play. Next was to standardize the flats and sharps, and to my surprise, that made a huge difference.

The final step was to experiment with the spacing, pulling the staves a bit further apart, making the measure look like a Henle edition. Now it was a luxury to read.

Essentially Arlen solved a practice issue by creating what we have called in this book a *practice part* (see chapter 4).

Hearing about his other practice technics, using practice parts created on his laptop to play back the music so the computer taught him the music, were eye-opening.

My conversations with Arlen changed my practice and led to new practice strategies with my students.

At the same time, I was continually referencing colleague and music educator Jennifer Mishra's research on memory and sight reading in my teaching and workshop presentations. Her topics of memorizing and sight reading are inevitably hot topics for pianists. And I know of no one else who explains research so easily to students, and who can make research easily relatable to the general public.

I broached Jennifer with the idea of conducting a research project with the New York Philharmonic, using the research question: How do you practice premieres when there are no aural models? See our published article in the journal *Music Performance Research*. That eventual project resulted in even more practice ideas to keep trying out with students. We presented this research at a conference and Norman Hirschy, editor with Oxford University Press, approached Jennifer and I about the possibility of writing a book after hearing one of our presentations.

And as the proverb goes, one thing leads to another, and eventually this book was born. It was fun to share ideas with Jennifer, a string player and music educator, intermixed with my personal perspective of a piano pedagogue with a double major in flute.

We hope that the practice ideas in this book, utilizing easily available technology, help solve that one measure, or many, that inevitably present themselves in all of our musical journeys.

—Barbara Fast, November 28, 2017

Acknowledgments

This book would not have been possible without the many people who contributed both directly and indirectly to its creation. The authors would like to thank all the musicians who generously shared their experiences and practice strategies with us and opened our eyes to new ways of teaching and practicing. We would especially like to thank Arlen Fast, who was the inspiration for the project. We would also like to thank Norman Hirschy, who saw something in our research that made him think this book was possible.

Also, a huge thank you to Barbara Fast's group piano and private piano students over the years, for being willing to try out new practice ideas. We are also indebted to the many talented graduate teaching assistants at the University of Oklahoma who have been willing to try out new ideas and give constant feedback regarding what worked and didn't work in the classroom.

We'd also like to thank Jennifer's husband Michael, who listened, edited, and generally provided mental health support during the creation of this book.

A number of music students and faculty contributed to this book who may not be directly referenced in the text: Liz Avery, Bailee Moore, Zac Cairns, Erika A. Cummings, Elise Fast, Jeongwon Ham, David J. Handy, David Howard, Marvin Lamb, Jane Magrath, Courtney Mantle, Amanda Shaw, Emily Truckenbrod, Kyle Vanderburg, Todd Van Kekerix, Irv Wagner, and the Honors Research Assistant Program at the University of Oklahoma.

About the Companion Website

www.oup.com/us/ipractice

Oxford has created a website to accompany *iPractice: Technology in the 21st Century Music Practice Room*. Material that cannot be made available in a book, namely complete interviews with musicians and teachers, reviews of relevant apps, video and audio tutorials, aural models of musical excerpts printed in the book, and full color versions of graphics printed in the book, are provided here. The reader is encouraged to consult this resource in conjunction with the chapters. Examples available online are indicated in the text with Oxford's symbol ▶.

Introduction

Overview of the Book

Through this book we intend to bridge the gap between the use of familiar, easy-to-use technology and musical practice to enhance musicianship and motivate students. The goal is to provide practical ideas for use with students of all levels, from those in book 1 to musicians performing advanced repertoire. This book is written for teachers (both studio teachers and ensemble directors), but it can be read through the lens of a performer guiding their own practice sessions. After all, teachers of musicians are performers themselves!

The ideas presented will range from using common technologies in new ways to introducing more innovative practice strategies that could only have been created alongside 21st-century technology. The strategies that we'll explore in this book simply lay the foundation for how technology can be used in the practice room. The ideas are intended to spark creativity. Teachers and students are encouraged to vary practice strategies in personal ways to fit their own studios or practice routines.

Technology will continue to evolve, as should our practice strategies. What the short history of digital technology has taught us is that what is current today will change tomorrow—often in unimaginable ways.

To future-proof this book, we have focused on the enduring practice strategies behind the technology. The current hardware and software that can be used to enact these practice strategies today are likely to change. We will provide examples based on current technology, but these are only a window into the strategy itself. Most of the examples of technology in this book were chosen because they were easy to use, well designed, and had some sort of stability. For the apps that we have chosen, there are often multiple substitutes that will accomplish the same goal. Teachers should feel free to explore the many options available. It's all about integrating the technology into an effective practice strategy.

In this book an emphasis has been placed on technology that can be used by a wide variety of musicians, from those with basic technology skills to those who are more comfortable with technology. The companion website to this book includes short, basic tutorials that demonstrate how various examples in the book were created. These also provide dynamic aural and visual versions of the practice examples notated in the text. The companion website also includes some complete interviews with teachers and performers, app reviews, and color versions of examples included in the book.

This book arises out of the authors' published research with musicians from a major American orchestra regarding how experts practice for premiers, and the subsequent application of this research into the private studio and classroom.[1] We also draw on findings from other researchers, including those studying practice and expertise development both in the area of music and sports psychology. We have also provided endnotes with further sources to explore for readers who are interested in the research perspective behind the ideas presented in the book.

Chapter 1 introduces the idea of integrating common, easy-to-use technologies into the music practice room. We lay the foundation for the book by exploring effective and efficient music practice strategies supported by research. Underlying our discussion is the theory of expert performance and deliberate practice. We explore distributed practice, marking parts, mapping, blocking chords, working with a metronome, changing rhythms, and mental practice. We also introduce several new practice strategies that have not yet become common, such as interleaving practice. Throughout the book we will focus on how to expand these quality practice strategies with technology.

Chapter 2, "Overlooked and Evolving Technology," begins with everyday technologies that are often overlooked as aides to musical practice. Familiar technologies, like the metronome, have been transformed and reinvented in the app explosion of the 21st century. We explore how metronome apps and metronome-like apps such as the Amazing Slow Downer have evolved and lead to new practice strategies. We move the discussion onto web-based tools, touching on interactive websites (e.g., SmartMusic, Sight Reading Factory) that encourage independent learning. We then explore practice strategies that focus on annotation (marking in music) both from a low-tech and high-tech perspective. This leads us into a discussion of digital sources like IMSLP and their growing acceptance into the concert hall.

In chapter 3, "And the Ears Have It!: Listening and Self Recording," we focus on practice strategies that incorporate recordings—both audio and video. We start with the benefits of listening to and playing along with recorded models, both published and teacher-created, and what a flipped classroom might look like in a music studio. We then move on to discuss the benefits of recording lessons and reflecting on home practice to solidify learning through blogging and vlogging, introducing "musical selfies" along the way. We finish by exploring recording as a performance activity, from recording dress rehearsals, auditions, and playing tests to the new trends of multimedia, hybrid, and digital performances, including live streaming.

Chapter 4, "Taking the Next Step: Using Notation Software in the Practice Room," introduces the concept of a *practice part* to address particularly difficult sections in the music. A practice part is created using notational software (e.g., Finale, Sibelius, MuseScore, Noteflight) to produce a working document based on the original printed music, but one that is unique to the individual performer. These re-notations of the music can include augmenting rhythms, using enharmonics, or altering clefs. The practice part may look different on the page, but will sound the same as the original. We then expand the idea of practice parts and explore arranging the music in some way to help students learn it more effectively or efficiently. Strategies include simplifying the music and creating personal etudes.

Finally, in chapter 5, "Beyond Four Walls: Practicing as a Social Activity," we discuss the benefits of utilizing social media to increase motivation and decrease students' practice isolation. First, we draw upon motivational concepts used frequently in exercise, sports, and games and apply these to musical practice. This includes using timing, list creation, and gaming apps to track practice. We then explore ways of harnessing social media (e.g., Instagram, Facebook) to help students become better musicians through virtual interactions with their peers by sharing musical selfies, creating practice stories, and using virtual practice partners. We conclude with how online teaching (distance education) can be strategically incorporated into a music studio or class setting.

This book is all about exploring musical practice through technology. We've had fun trying out new ways of integrating technology in our own practice and with our students in studios and classrooms. We hope these ideas invigorate your musical practice and lead to even more creativity between you and your students.

Note

1. The research study on which this book is based was written by Jennifer Mishra and Barbara Fast and is titled "Practising in the New World: A Case Study of Practising Strategies Related to the Premiere of Contemporary Music." The article may be found in the journal *Music Performance Research*.

1

Bringing Practice into the 21st Century

Introduction

"Put your cell phone away!"

This is the call of teachers everywhere as they try to pry students' attention away from their mobile devices long enough to learn. In this book we propose another approach: integrating technology into musical practice. When technology is used specifically and intentionally, it expands traditional music practice techniques and allows students to engage in more self-directed learning.

Technology has been a whirlwind of change. Email only became common in the late 1990s and the iTunes app store went online in 2008, setting off the app explosion.[1] Even our very language changed, as we now "google" information or instruction.[2] We've all had to navigate this changing world and adapt to the growing technology in our daily lives, using it for everything from communication to entertainment. We continue to learn more with each computer or phone upgrade.[3]

Simply put, technology has become integrated into the very fabric of our daily lives.

Musicians by and large have not realized the full potential of using their personal tech devices (e.g., smartphones, tablets, or computers) in their own practicing and teaching. Some music teachers have been quick to adapt the ever-changing technology, while others have taken a wait-and-see approach, knowing that technology is constantly evolving. Some even fear technology may take away from the rich pedagogical traditions developed over centuries. After all, musicians have successfully practiced for hundreds of years without technology, and music has pedagogical techniques that date back a millennium (e.g., solfège).[4]

It's worth remembering that there is a history of musicians evolving their practice strategies as new technologies became available. The metronome (invented in 1815),[5] for instance, was quickly promoted by many composers and ultimately established new methods of practice. Smartphones, tablets, and computers have the potential of similarly creating new practice strategies for a new generation. Rather than taking away from pedagogical traditions developed in the 19th century, technology broadens the possibilities available and allows new creative practice techniques to emerge—adding more tools to the practice toolbox.

Teachers may assume that students—especially millennials, who grew up with technology—will easily transfer everyday technology into their own musical practice. Surprisingly, this is often not the case.[6] As with any practice strategy, students need guidance to make appropriate choices and practice strategies using technology are no different. It's important for teachers to guide and model effective strategies using technology.

Today's technology can literally transform the way we approach musical practice and teaching. It can be liberating for both students and teachers to embrace their own tech devices to assist in practicing and teaching.

Instead of "Put your cell phone away," the rallying cry for music teachers can instead be "Keep your cell phones out!"

But before we jump into the technology, let's start with a brief summary of several key practice strategies supported by research both in music and sports psychology. Many of the quality practice techniques discussed below will be revisited in later chapters through the lens of technology.

Let's practice!

Underlying this book is the theory of expert performance based on the research of K. Anders Ericsson and colleagues.[7] This theory focuses on developing expertise through practice and experience, and is less concerned with talent. It is practice and hard work that tends to lead to success rather than natural, innate abilities. Ten thousand hours is the number often cited to achieve expertise in an area, though this is just a general rule of thumb popularized by Malcolm Gladwell in his book *Outliers*.[8]

But it's not just *any* practice or experience that leads to success; it's *deliberate, mindful* practice. Mindless physical repetition has limited usefulness. Research has shown that experts across many fields, including music, engage in deliberate preparation, planning, reasoning, and evaluation when performing.[9] In short, it is the quality of practice that counts more than quantity.

Research shows that "novice musicians have problems identifying difficult sections and tend to practice by simply playing through the music."[10] Teachers must guide the students to be more effective and efficient practicers.[11] This applies to both children and adult learners.[12]

There are individual preferences when it comes to practice strategies, and the type and scope may vary depending on the expertise level of the musician. What follows is an exploration of practice strategies emphasizing deliberate, thoughtful practice. Many of these are familiar, tried-and-true practice strategies. Others may be more unfamiliar to teachers and students.

Practice: space it out and mix it up

The first decision that needs to be made in practicing is *when* to practice. Again and again, research has found that distributing practice over time is beneficial to learning.[13] Cramming (what the psychologists call "massed practice") is intensive learning over a short period of time with no rest breaks. This can lead to short-term learning, but the material learned isn't stable. Students are frequently surprised by how much music they don't retain after intensive practice. Distributing practice over time results in more reliable long-term learning.

For musicians, this means scheduling practice sessions over time with opportunities to rest in between. Practice can be distributed in multiple ways: over weeks, throughout the course of a day, and even within one practice session.

Long-term distributed practice

Teachers have long recommended spacing out practicing between lessons. For instance, shorter practice sessions over five days is far more effective than longer practice sessions over one or two days.[14] We all know students who leave practicing to the day before the lesson and then can't quite understand why their playing doesn't improve!

Yes, we're talking about the students who procrastinate.

The principle behind distributed practice is that over time students forget just a little bit of what they initially learned. They have to go through a brief relearning process every time they practice, and this relearning process is what helps the material stick.

Distributing practice over time also helps keep the musician's mind alert. There's a limit to the amount of attention performers have available in one practice session. Younger students have shorter attention spans than adults, but even adults can't practice indefinitely; they become mentally (and possibly also physically) fatigued. Even a brief break allows the mind and body to recharge.

There's actually no hard-and-fast rule about how much students should practice. This depends on the student's level and attention span, as well as the music they are working on. In general, pianists practice more than string players, who tend to practice more than wind players, and practice time increases with age.[15] In summary, it's not just about how much time a student practices, but how the time is distributed that counts.

Daily distributed practice

What is less well known is that spacing out practice during the day is more effective than one longer practice session. Resting or sleeping between practice sessions helps musicians consolidate learning.[16]

BOX 1.1 From a performer

I tell people to divide practice up. Never do more than an hour and a half without stopping and giving yourself a break. For two reasons: physically, you don't want to tire certain elements and get tendonitis or whatever. Secondly, your brain freezes over after a certain amount and you lose perspective and lose perception on what you're actually doing. If you repeat, your fingers get tired and then your brain begins to not know if you're improving.

I tell students, do an hour and a half in the morning and do an hour and a half in the afternoon or evening. Or put an hour and a half in the afternoon and do another hour and a half in the evening. Break it up. And you'll come up fresher and you'll be revived.

Second thing is don't practice the same thing for an hour. Practice it for 10–15 minutes and then switch to something else. Switch to another piece or another etude or another scale or whatever you're perfecting, stop perfecting it after fifteen minutes cause it won't get any better. And also, try to divide your practice time and finish the last ten minutes, play something you enjoy playing, give yourself a nice reward at the end of your practice time.

—Orin O'Brien, bassist, New York Philharmonic[17]

In the quote in Box 1.1, Orin O'Brien advocates distributing practice throughout the day, but she also advocates switching to different sections or pieces throughout the course of one practice session. This idea has support from cognitive and sports psychology and is called *interleaving practice*.

Interleaving practice

There are many ways of organizing practice sessions. Probably the most common way is to block practice—focusing attention on one piece or technically difficult section within a piece before moving to a completely different piece or section. Another way, suggested by educators and psychologists, is to interleave practice—returning to a piece or a section of a piece repeatedly throughout one practice session, while in between practicing another passage.[18]

As the English proverb says: "A change is as good as a rest."[19]

Figure 1.1 visually represents block practice (example A) and interleaving practice (example B) over the same amount of time. The difference is how the time is structured. In the example, A may represent an entire section of a piece or just a few measures. Interleaving practice doesn't necessarily have to be in a specific order (example C); the strategy is more about alternating shorter practice segments in a less structured way.

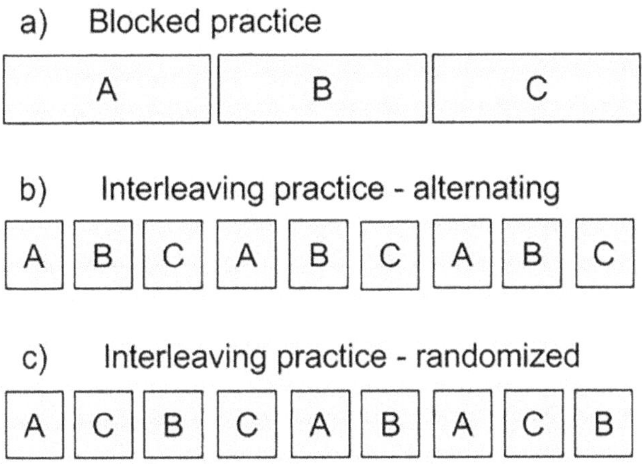

FIGURE 1.1 Diagrams representing three different practicing activities (A, B, and C) arranged in a blocked practice session (example A), an alternating interleaving practice session (example B), and a randomized interleaving practice session (example C).

Interleaving practice may not seem intuitive, but as with other forms of distributed practice, returning to the material keeps the passage fresh and reduces mindless practice that sometimes sets in with fatigue. Interleaving practice is deliberate and mindful. With each return to a passage, there is a brief relearning process while the brain remembers previously learned material.

Interleaving practice can be accomplished in one of two ways: 1) placing a time limit on practicing with each segment getting a fixed amount of time, or 2) practicing until a passage feels completed and returning to that passage later in the practice session to check learning. The important aspect of both scenarios is that the passage is returned to within the same practice session maybe even three or four times.

The length of the passage doesn't matter. Beginning level students might alternate one-measure segments (e.g., measure 1 with measure 4). Beginning and intermediate students may need a teacher's assistance in choosing appropriate practice segments to alternate. Advanced students will likely be more independent in identifying technical challenges to rotate.

Table 1.1 shows an example of what blocked practice versus interleaved practice might look like, based on a research study by Christine Carter and Jessica Grahn.[20] Notice that the practice time is the same in both columns for the concerto and the technical study, but in the interleaved schedule column, the concerto was practiced in four short, three-minute practice sessions versus one twelve-minute block.

The interleaved schedule resulted in better performances. However, students discounted this strategy in favor of the blocked schedule. Possibly the blocked schedule felt more focused and like more progress was being made. In reality, the quick benefits of block practice disappear quickly.

TABLE 1.1 Practice time organized in a block schedule and an interleaved schedule.

	Block Schedule		Interleaved Schedule
3 minutes	Read concerto exposition	3 minutes	Read concerto exposition
12 minutes	Practice concerto exposition	1 minute	Read technical study
1 minute	Read technical study	3 minutes	Practice concerto exposition
12 minutes	Practice technical study	3 minutes	Practice technical study
		3 minutes	Practice concerto exposition
		3 minutes	Practice technical study
		3 minutes	Practice concerto exposition
		3 minutes	Practice technical study
		3 minutes	Practice concerto exposition
		3 minutes	Practice technical study
28 minutes	Total Practice Time	28 minutes	Total Practice Time

Adapted from a research study conducted by Christine Carter and Jessica Grahn (2016). Used by permission.

After working with this strategy, some students are able to see the benefits of interleaving practice. Box 1.2 includes some reactions from a doctoral student pianist who has been using interleaving practice for several years.

Before we leave interleaving practice, let's introduce the concept of interleaved *teaching*. During the course of a lesson or a class, the teacher moves on and then returns to a passage or idea. This circling back around is particularly effective with short, technical drill work or when introducing a new concept. The trick is knowing when to move on and then remembering to return to the passage or idea later in the lesson.

Distributing practice, whether it be over the course of one practice session or throughout the week, takes thought and planning, but the long-term payoffs can be enormous.

Chunking: finding the patterns

Many effective practice strategies work because they help us simplify music that appears to be complex. Grouping individual pieces of information (like notes or rhythms) into meaningful patterns is called "chunking" in psychology.[21] Finding patterns in the music will make learning faster and much more efficient.[22] After all, music is mostly repetition with variation—patterns are everywhere, in rhythm, pitch, harmony, and form.

Research on pattern recognition tells us that experts and beginners perceive patterns differently. In fact, one of the defining characteristics of an expert seems to

BOX 1.2 From a doctoral student

A lot of the time when we sit down to practice and we're not focused, our mind wanders. We tend to just give ourselves our own private concert.

With interleaving, or segmented practice as I call it, I rotate working between two passages. I've done it with as many as three or four different segments in the music. I'll work for ten minutes on a passage, and sometimes only five minutes if I'm rotating between several passages.

With interleaved practice, or any practice in short segments, you're able to be more focused because the amount of time you are spending on it is so short.

Those chunks of time really add up, and they can be very mentally exhausting. I typically never do more than thirty or forty-five minutes of interleaved practice at one time. By then the focus starts to wear off, and this type of practice is only useful if you are focused 100 percent the entire time.

The biggest benefit of interleaving practice is the process of having to switch back and forth. The solutions are implemented much more quickly than if I kept practicing the same thing over and over again. I've found that fewer repetitions that are higher quality and spread out force the brain to recall things more accurately.

—Omar Roy, pianist

BOX 1.3 Visit the companion website

▶ For a full interview with Omar Roy describing the use of interleaving practice in his practicing and teaching, see the companion website 1.1.

be that they can recognize patterns.[23] Patterns seem obvious to music teachers who are musical experts, but students may need guidance to see these patterns. It's worth spending lesson time helping the student find patterns. What the practice strategies in this section have in common is that they all, in their own way, help students find patterns in the music.

Marking parts: circling and labeling

Sometimes students dive right into practicing without a full understanding of the piece. Score analysis, at its root, is simply seeing patterns in the music. These patterns can be personal—in other words, they don't need to be "right" in a music theory sense. Patterns

The Many Ways of Marking Parts

Form

Marking repetition (same and different) with letters, brackets, circles, or parentheses.

Measure Numbers

Many scores include printed measure numbers, but others do not. Measure numbers simplifies communication between student and teacher throughout the learning process.

Beats & Meter Indicating beats using slashes (vertical lines) above or through the notes simplifies rhythmically complex music and provides visual landmarks. These help the performer track the pulse through music. For quickly changing meter, it helps to add a graphic symbol that represents a conductor's beat pattern (e.g., triangle for ¾)

Phrase Markings & Slurs help visually organize the music. Slurs frequently identify articulations and bow changes for strings. For singers slurs may indicate portamentos or melismas. Phrase markings may encompass a larger group of notes than a slur.

Part Identification Musicians reading from parts that contain multiple lines (e.g., choral score, divisi) sometimes indicate the part they are to play or sing with arrows, stars, or other labels including highlighting part.

Translations Singers may write in a word for word translation when singing in a foreign language.

Pedaling Young students frequently need direction for when to use the pedal or in making pedaling decisions. Pedaling decisions are made by the ear, but putting in pedal markings as reminders, to emphasize harmony, phrasing or rhythm can be a helpful learning tool.

Metronome Markings

If not already included in the printed edition, metronome markings can be written in at the beginning of the piece and where there are large tempo changes. These provide students with concrete performance goals.

Pitch Adjustments Arrows are often used to indicate notes on instruments that are inherently flat or sharp or pitches that need to be raised or lowered depending on where the pitch lies in a chord.

Dynamics are often printed in the music, but performers may wish to modify or add dynamics as reminders or to better show a particular interpretation. Including dynamics at the beginning of the learning process helps students integrate the physical motions needed to perform musically.

Cues Editors often include cues in ensemble music. Performers may write in additional cues either in the form of notated music, rhythms, or written reminders (e.g., "Horn entrance").

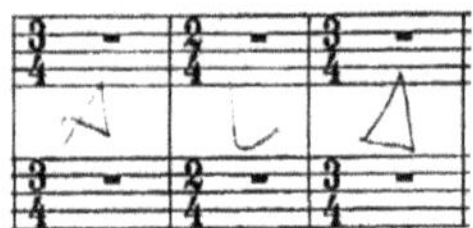

Reminders & Attention Grabbers

Performers may write one or two words to remember interpretive decisions. These can be analogies, imagery (e.g., "sounds like rain") or descriptive words (e.g., "lighter"), and may be meaningful only to the individual performer

Breath Marks

An apostrophe in the music indications where to breath. Other musicians (e.g., string players) also organize breathing to coordinate playing or to indicate a brief pause in the flow of the music, sometimes accompanied by a bowing change.

FIGURE 1.2 Visual overview of the various ways musicians may mark parts and scores during practice.

The Many Ways of Marking Parts (Cont'd)

Navigation & Directions

Performers may write in navigational reminders such as when to turn the page ("V. S." or "Turn") or write in measures just before or after an awkward page turn or to remember how many measures of rest. Navigational reminders may also include circles, brackets, or arrows to indicate repeats, D.S., codas, cuts, etc. Cuts (*vide*) may be indicated with a "vi---" at the start of the cut and "---de" at the end of the cut.

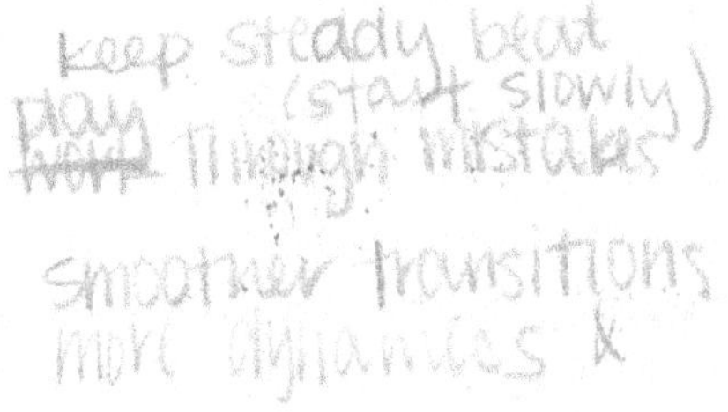

Pronunciations

Singers especially when singing in a foreign language, may write in phonetic pronunciations for the lyrics (IPA) or placement of consonants.

Chords

Labeling a chord or tonal progression simplifies a passage especially.

Articulations

Markings used for articulations (dots, dashes, accent marks, etc.) are often general indications of the desired sound. Most articulations can be played in multiple ways depending on the style of the piece, dynamics, personal interpretation, etc

Practice Goals may be written in list form or take the form of asterisks, circles, or check marks by lines/passages that need intensive work. Progress may also be noted related to tempo (current playable metronome marking for passage).

Rubato markings indicate where to take time or move ahead in the music. There are numerous rubato markings including: squiggly lines, arrows, *ten.*, caesuras (i.e.., "railroad tracks", //), spectacles, etc.

Stickings & Tonguing

Percussionists may indicate the left and right hand coordination of a passage (e.g., LRLL) and brass and woodwind players sometimes indicate tonguing marks frequently using the letters T and K.

Fingerings There are often various options for fingerings, but it is important to solidify fingering choices early in the learning process as it is fundamental to consistency in performance. String players sometimes use arrows above the notation as a reminder of finger placement (e.g., low 2nd finger). String players may also mark in positions or which string to play on using Roman numerals.

Bowings/Slurs String players write in bowings to indicate which direction the bow should be traveling. String players also may indicate which part of the bow to play (e.g., tip).

Rhythmic Counting (e.g., 1e&a) is a way of helping students keep track of where they are in a measure. Asking students to write in counting emphasizes sub-divisions and allows teachers to assess whether students are trying to play the passage by ear.

Pitches & Relationships Pitch names may be added to a note especially when multiple ledger lines are present or an important or target note circled. Symbols such as a connecting line or half-step marking indicate how one pitch relates to another.

FIGURE 1.3 Visual overview (continued) of the various ways musicians may mark parts and scores during practice.

only need to make sense to the performer. Marking and labeling these patterns in the music helps visually highlight similarities and differences.

Performers have preferences as to how much or how little to mark in the music. One approach is to mark all decisions in the music and then systematically remove markings as they are no longer necessary. Another approach is to write in only the absolutely necessary markings needed to remember decisions. See Figures 1.2 and 1.3 for a descriptive list of possible markings.

Form in particular is important; it's a way of seeing the big picture—the organization of the piece. Form need not be difficult or advanced—it's just a matter of finding same and different. This applies equally to an easy eight-measure piece or a Beethoven sonata.

When practicing, encourage students to practice similar sections together even if they are separated within the piece. After all, once the first passage has been practiced, any repetition of the passage (or variation on the passage) is now a review. Practice becomes more efficient. The brain isn't learning the repeated passage as a new passage. It is key for the teacher to help students recognize and mark any patterns in the music. Students often overlook patterns that seem obvious to the teacher.

Mapping

Creating a visual map or representation of a piece can be particularly useful for simplifying and clarifying the patterns in large works. Rebecca Shockley's book *Mapping Music: For Faster Learning and Secure Memory* focuses on this technique, which she calls "mapping."[24] In essence, students create a visual representation of the piece with simple patterns—lines, curves, shapes, slash patterns, or whatever makes sense to the performer. The important part is that the similar passages are represented visually in a similar way.

Mapping can be used with young students at a very basic level or older students performing more complex repertoire. The important part is to condense the entire piece into a one-page visual map using symbols that make sense to the performer. This helps students identify when passages are similar and different, information that can be used when organizing practice. Figure 1.4 shows an example of a student-created map of the piece "A Quiet Lagoon," a beginner-level piano piece.[25]

Score analysis may be different depending on whether the piece is a solo, chamber, or orchestral work. But the idea of understanding the purpose of any given line or section and how it fits into the whole applies to all music, as Eric Bartlett reminds us in Box 1.5.

Sometimes teachers assume that students have made key decisions early, but inconsistency or a hiccup in performance reveals weak (or lack of) decision-making. Research shows that expert musicians make musical decisions very early in the learning process.[26] Making these decisions may seem tedious to students, and so they need guidance in making important decisions such as fingerings. Writing the decisions into the part solidifies them for future practice. It's also important at this point to look for any similar

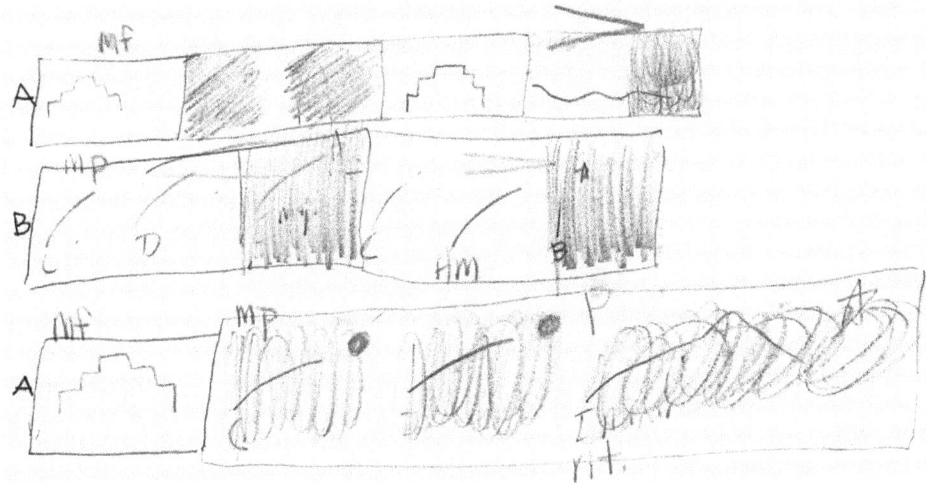

FIGURE 1.4 A student-created map for the beginning-level piano piece "A Quiet Lagoon." Piano teacher Joy Morin discusses the creation of this map on her blog *Color in My Piano*. Example used by permission of Joy Morin.

BOX 1.4 Visit the companion website

Visit the companion website 1.2 and 1.3 for a full color version of the chart "The Many Ways of Marking Parts."

BOX 1.5 From a performer

I'm always filling my part with little cues, not just in new music. For the newer music, I'll get a score and I'll actually sit with the score and a part and put in many cues, if there is room to do so. If not, I'll go back to the score and make my own cut and paste. I might do a cut and paste in which I can see the violin part throughout a whole movement or section, and then do cues for a section that is rhythmically less complicated. However you get there, you just *have* to know what's going on.

—Eric Bartlett, cellist, New York Philharmonic[27]

passages and transfer the markings to the repeated passages. Sometimes simply making a definite decision allows the student to play the passage without further practice.

Blocking chords

Blocking chords is a valuable practice strategy for pianists and other multivoiced instruments (e.g., guitar, marimba). Music is full of chord patterns, but these chord patterns are not always easy to recognize because the notes are not played at the same time or are interspersed with other notes. Blocking chords (playing the chord tones at the same time) is a way of visually and physically simplifying the basic outline of the chord structure. The pattern becomes simple to play once it's recognized.

Figure 1.5 shows an example of a piece where the left hand plays a traditional alberti bass pattern (chord tones are played in a running eighth note pattern). By taking out the rhythm and playing all of the chord tones at the same time (blocked), the chordal movement becomes clear and is easy to learn.

The process of blocking chords is a mental simplification process; it reduces perceived complexity. Blocking chords allows students to quickly gain a mental and physical overview of the piece. Some pieces are really very simple once the chords are blocked since they require surprisingly few hand positions for the entire piece.

Though blocking chords works best with multivoiced instruments, finding the chord structure can be helpful for other instruments even if the notes can't technically be played at the same time. In Figure 1.6, the Bach's Prelude from *Suite No. 1 for Solo Cello in G Major,* each measure is just one chord with one hand shape (G, C, f#-dim with a pedal, G).

FIGURE 1.5 Notation for measures 1–4 of Mozart's *Piano Sonata*, K. 545, 1st movement, showing the original score (example A) and simplified blocked chords for the left hand created in a notation program (example B). To listen to this example, please go to the companion website 1.1.

BOX 1.6 Visit the companion website

Go to the companion website 1.4 to hear measures 1–4 of Mozart's *Piano Sonata*, K. 545, 1st movement as written and with simplified blocked chords in the left hand created in Noteflight.

FIGURE 1.6 Notation for measures 1–4 of Bach's *Suite No. 1 for Solo Cello in G Major*, BWV 1007, Prelude, showing the original score (example A) and simplified blocked chords created in a notation program (example B). To listen to this example, please go to the companion website 1.2.

> **BOX 1.7 Visit the companion website**
>
> Go to the companion website 1.5 to hear measures 1–4 of M Bach's *Cello Suite No. 1 in G Major*, MWV 1007, prelude as written and with simplified blocked chords created in Noteflight.

Knowing this helps the performer place fingers on the instrument. It also helps the performer memorize the piece since one chord is easier to remember than sixteen individual notes.

Circling and labeling groups of notes (chords, scales, arpeggios, motives, etc.) as a unit helps conceptualize music in a simpler way. In reality, any group of notes may form a meaningful pattern if the performer sees the unit as connected. Performers may even find patterns in aleatoric (random) music just as we see patterns in the stars and label them as constellations.

Perceiving, circling, and labeling underlying musical patterns takes very little time, but is an easy practice step to ignore. Once the patterns are identified, it's time to get back to the instrument and put the fingers to work.

Divide and conquer

Woodshedding is the term used by musicians to indicate intensive practice on short difficult sections. Left to their own devices, students frequently have difficulty identifying difficult passages and using strategies to effectively conquer them. They often just want to play through the entire piece over and over.[28]

But repetition on it's own is not a practice strategy—at least not a very efficient one. Playing through a piece may feel satisfying, but this actually delays learning because students gloss over problem passages.

The process of woodshedding starts with an overview of the section or piece to determine what needs the most immediate work, followed by intensive practice (woodshedding) of that particular small section, finally playing the piece or section in context to see if the difficult passage sticks.[29] This process in education is sometimes called the "whole-part-whole" method, also referred to as "learning sequences" or "sequential patterns of instruction" when used in a rehearsal context.

The strategies described in the next section help students identify and isolate problem passages in order to conquer them.

Hardest first

Musicians tend to focus practice on what is most comfortable and familiar—even if they don't realize it.[30] The tendency is to begin at the beginning of the piece and avoid the more difficult sections that typically occur in the middle or the end of the work. To counter this, one option is to begin practicing at the end, with the last phrase, and move forward—building the piece backward. Another option is to practice the hardest passages first.

Practicing the hardest first means identifying the most challenging few measures or sections of music and practice these passages first. The length of the section chosen for practice depends on the difficulty of the passage, but in general, the more complex the passage, the smaller the section chosen.[31] Once small sections have been mastered, they can be hooked together to form longer sections—building the piece from the inside out.

But don't forget to practice transitions into and out of the passage![32] These are easily forgotten and not necessarily natural to practice.

Teachers will likely need to help students identify the hardest passages by marking these in the music and setting practice goals. In a lesson or rehearsal, starting at the beginning of a piece to establish context and style is important, but teacher should help students focus on difficult passages by giving them priority early in the learning process.

Building it up: metronome practice

The metronome was a new technology in the early 19th century and changed the way musicians practiced. Today, using a metronome is one of the most advocated practice strategies.[33] Not all teachers agree on how much the metronome should be used; some insist on constant use while others use it more sparingly, emphasizing inner pulse over the external pulse of the metronome. However, most agree that the metronome has its place, especially when woodshedding difficult, fast passages.

Practicing with a metronome means starting at a slow, playable tempo and gradually increasing the tempo—two ticks at a time or ten—with performance tempo as the goal. Musicians often describe this process as "building it up" or "digging it out"—imagery that emphasizes the work involved. The numerical feedback structuring this practice strategy can be motivational and sometimes addictive. It's a numerical way of keeping score, much like a Fitbit keeps track of steps.

Metronomes allow us to measure where we are versus where we are going.

Using a metronome is such a simple practice strategy, but students can sometimes make key mistakes. They often begin too fast and sometimes get ahead of themselves, moving up the speed too quickly and not stabilizing the performance at a particular tempo. To ensure stability, performers often create rules for themselves such as playing the passage three or five times in a row without error.

Teachers can prepare students to effectively use the metronome by describing the common problems that may emerge. For instance, students will likely hit plateaus—a point at which they can't play any faster—as they speed up the tempo. Rather than becoming frustrated and continuing, unsuccessfully, to practice at the plateau tempo, students should instead slow down the tempo and build it up again. This seems like going backward, but the build up is usually quicker the second (or third) time and students can usually push past the plateau.

There is also the danger of getting stuck in too much slow practice. Different muscle motions or gestures are used when playing passages slow and fast—sometimes limiting transfer to fast passage work. Playing at a faster tempo, even if a note or two is dropped, encourages the natural gesture, embouchure, or breathing that the quicker tempo demands. It is not uncommon for musicians to rethink technical or expressive decisions once they are performing at tempo. Sometimes after practicing slowly with a metronome, there comes a time when the student should set the metronome at or near performance tempo and simply go for it! In Box 1.8, John McGrosso describes why it might not always be a good idea to start with the metronome at a slow tempo.

BOX 1.8 From a teacher and performer

One problem I find is that as string students start learning fast passages slowly, they choreograph their motions at those slower tempos. The more time they spend playing slowly, the more that this inefficient choreography becomes ingrained. These inefficiencies (using too much bow, not anticipating string crossings, squeezing before shifts) will all cause problems as they get closer to their performance tempo. But by practicing in short bursts but in a tempo closer to that of the performance, students can understand sooner how they will need to move in the performance tempo, and then solve the problems they will actually face in the concert. No amount of walking teaches you to run; running and walking are completely different physical experiences. Playing faster sooner will teach students where the inefficiencies are in their playing, and this awareness of efficiency improves their slow playing as well.

There is also a different listening that has to take place when playing fast passages. Some of my most conscientious students try to listen to each note as they are playing to make sure each one is in its place, but as they try to go faster and faster, that kind of "backward listening" isn't so helpful. With fast passages, I encourage them to focus on their physical motion as they are playing, and to listen to the effect of the total passage almost in retrospect. Then, they can experiment with adjustments to their motions that improve their result the next time. Playing faster sooner, or at least mixing fast playing into slow practicing, can also help students avoid the problem of too much left-hand tension; if they experience having to move through a passage faster they will not have time to build in so much pressure. When people run quickly, only their toes touch the ground; we can learn a lot from this.

—John McGrosso, violinist, Arianna String Quartet

BOX 1.9 Visit the companion website

Listen to the interview with violinist and teacher John McGrosso on the companion website 1.6, which includes musical demonstrations.

Even if the entire passage can't be played at tempo, students can perform smaller chunks at tempo. In Figure 1.7, which starts the fugal passage of the Scherzo in Beethoven's *Symphony No. 9*, the violins begin with a quick rhythmic gesture. The physical motion becomes different if played at a slower tempo. To preserve the correct physical motion, it is more efficient to practice smaller chunks of the musical motive at tempo and then join the chunks together.

For instance in Figure 1.7, students can play one measure into the downbeat of the next, and then pause before playing the next measure (example A). When this is comfortable, measures can be strung together for a longer gesture (example B).

The hands physically experience the faster tempo, even if it's just for one measure. This is another way of practicing the building up of a passage at a fast tempo rather than a slow tempo.

Interspersing fast with slow practice, guided by the metronome, is a helpful way of checking progress and keeps the passage fresh. Students benefit from a period of fast practice even when they are still working up the passage. This will also help students to not get bogged down in slow practice. Once performance tempo is established, briefly returning to slow practice keeps technique clean.

Using the metronome is a systematic process that imposes a discipline onto the practice. This strategy allows students to easily measure achievement and accomplish evolving performance goals on their way to a final performance tempo. If done well, the student should always feel successful—at whatever tempo they are playing.

Digging it out: woodshedding strategies

Problems occurring in difficult passages often need special practice strategies to solve. As discussed earlier, one of the most common ways of practicing a difficult section is to slow

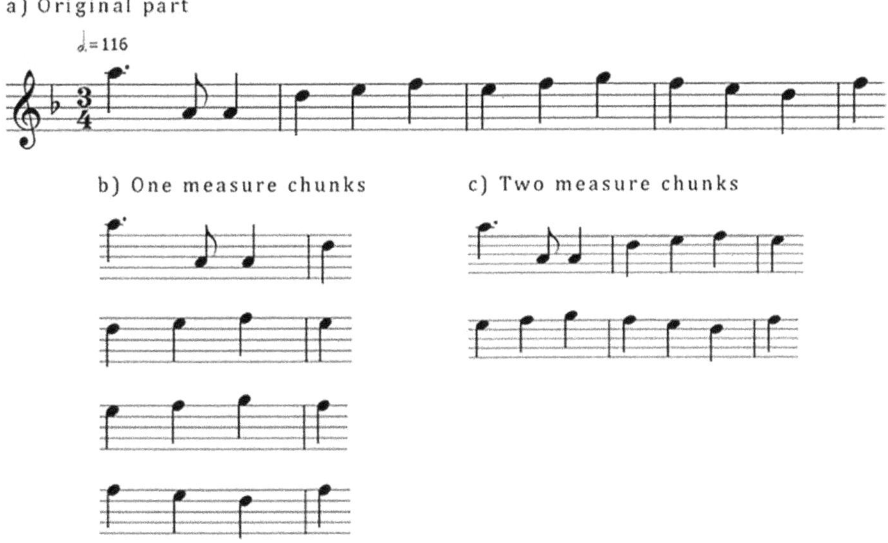

FIGURE 1.7 Notation for measures 9–13 of Beethoven's *Symphony No. 9*, 2nd movement, Violin I part, showing the original score (example A), practicing in one-measure chunks at tempo (example B), and practicing in two-measure chunks at tempo (example C). Created in a notation program. To listen to this example, please go to the companion website.

it down and then build it back up to performance tempo with a metronome, but there are other ways to tackle a difficult section.

A particularly helpful practice strategy is to focus attention on only one element of music, such as melody or rhythm, isolating a difficult rhythm on only one pitch or playing challenging melodies in half or whole notes. There are many creative ways to approach this practice strategy, as Arlen Fast describes in Box 1.10. String players may practice open strings and string crossings without fingering the pitches, and pianists can practice hands separately. Even expert performers use this strategy.

Let's return to the first measure of Bach's *Suite No. 1 for Solo Cello in G Major*, an example from earlier in the chapter, to see how these strategies might look if notated. Many student cellists struggle with playing the sixteenth notes consistently and smoothly over the string crossings (note: slurs have been left out, as string players have many different ways of bowing the passage). Figure 1.8 shows three simple ways of changing the rhythmic pattern: adding repeated notes; imposing a rhythmic pattern (e.g., short-long or long-short); and adding accents (e.g., groups of 3, 4, or 5) to a series of notes. Changing rhythms or imposing accents to add variation to a melodic line can highlight weaknesses in technique and can actually make the original passage seem easier by comparison.

Another strategy to shake things up during woodshedding is to "play opposites." For instance, play a *forte* passage *piano* (reversed dynamics), play staccato passages legato (reversed articulations), or play fast passages slow or slow passages fast (reversed tempo).

BOX 1.10 From a performer

A lot of times, addressing a technical problem is easiest if you simply separate out all the different issues so you can work on them one at a time. For example, you can take out changes of notes so you can focus on the rhythm. Playing the rhythm using only one note allows you to internalize it more easily. Or, you can take out rhythm and just play the sequences of notes until the fingers get used to them. This makes it easier to identify and work on particularly difficult note changes or sequences within a passage. Just don't worry about rhythm until the fingers know where they are going, and the ear gets used to the progression. Also, early on you can leave dynamics and other markings out until you are really ready to integrate them. Just deal with one thing at a time and add one thing at a time into the mix. Building a passage stepwise is the easiest thing for me because that way I'm only having to contend with one new thing at a time.

—Arlen Fast, bassoonist, New York Philharmonic[34]

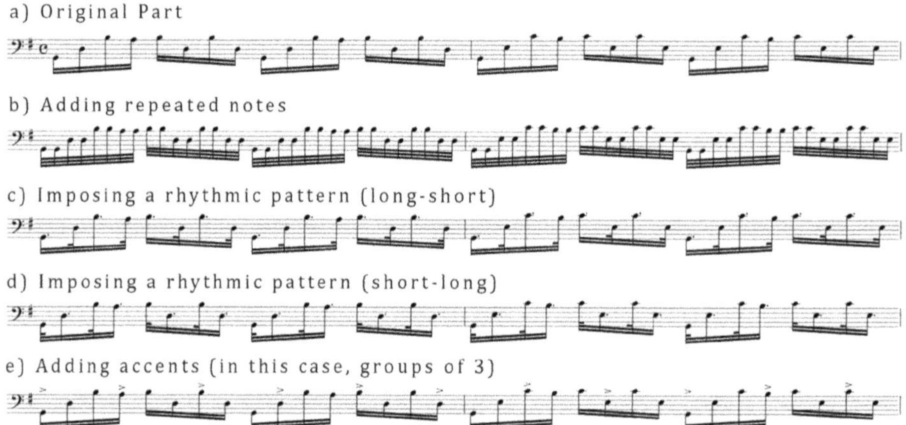

FIGURE 1.8 Notation for measure 1–2 of Bach's *Suite No. 1 for Solo Cello in G Major*, BWV 1007, Prelude, showing the original score (example A), adding repeated 32nd notes (example B), imposing a rhythmic pattern of long-short (example C), imposing a rhythmic pattern of short-long (example D), and adding accents in groups of three (example E). Created in a notation program. To listen to this example, please go to the companion website.

Shadow playing or pretend playing is another version of removing one element to simplify the learning process. Young string players are sometimes encouraged to shadow bow passages with the bow either on the top of the violin or in the crook of the elbow. Similarly, pianists can pretend to play the piece on the keyboard cover ("table-top playing"). A more difficult version of this is to play one hand on the keyboard and one hand pretend-playing on the upper ledge of the piano. This allows finger technique to solidify without being hampered by hearing incorrect notes.

These woodshedding strategies vary the approach to difficult passages, allowing students to experience the passage in a new way.

But wait! We're not done practicing!

Woodshedding strategies assist performers in isolating and dissecting problems in minute detail, but the final step—an important step—is to put the music back together. Play the difficult passage in its musical context. Students tend to feel that they don't need to put the music back together again, but this is an essential step in the learning process. Mentally, this allows for consolidation and an assessment of where the passage now stands.

Mental practice

An underutilized practice strategy is *visualization* or mental practice. This is used heavily in the sports world, and can easily be adapted to music.[35] In essence, visualizing is mentally imagining playing away from the instrument. This strategy takes away the physical motions of performing and forces the musician to internalize the sound and visualize the motions needed to perform the music.

Many musicians may use this strategy when preparing for performance. The point is to visualize every aspect of the performance including the venue, pre-performance rituals, and stage presence (e.g., bowing). An alternative approach is for the musician to imagine being part of the audience, watching their own successful performance.

This visualization strategy works equally well when learning a piece. This may not seem like practice, but there is neurological basis for improved performance. The brain processes imagined movements in a similar way to actual movements (the term used in psychology is "mirror neurons").[36]

This means that practicing doesn't have to stop because of physical fatigue or when playing an instrument isn't an option (e.g., when a piano isn't available or volume may be too loud for neighbors). Visualization can also be particularly useful when the performer has a physical limitation (e.g., injury) and can be used to extend practice beyond what is physically recommended.

Visualization is a powerful tool that can be embedded into a regular practice routine by alternating physical and mental practice. This type of mental practice takes a lot of effort and may naturally slow down the imagined tempo. Eventually, with practice, the visualized tempo will match the performance tempo.

Conclusion

We'll revisit and expand upon the practice strategies we've discussed in this chapter using technology, but before we do, one last thought about practicing in general.

Research shows that students tend to be more influenced by what a teacher does in his or her lesson than any practice advice. Good home practicing begins with thoughtful lesson planning and modeling. It's important to demonstrate quality practice strategies in the lessons in order for students to use these strategies at home.[37]

This book is about a more colorful palette of practice strategies using technology. The practice strategies described in this chapter are a foundation for what is to come.

Now, it's time for some technology. So, here we go!

Notes

1. For a brief history of email and mobile technology, see Ray Tomlinson's article "How Did Email Grow from Messages Between Academics to a Global Epidemic?" in *The Guardian*, March 7, 2016, www.theguardian.com/technology/2016/mar/07/email-ray-tomlinson-history and Matt Strain's article "1983 to Today: A History of Mobile Apps" in *The Guardian*, February 13, 2015, www.theguardian.com/media-network/2015/feb/13/history-mobile-apps-future-interactive-timeline.
2. "Google," *Dictionary.com Unabridged*, www.dictionary.com/browse/google.
3. For readers interested in the evolution of musical recording technology, see *Capturing Sound* by Mark Katz.
4. Susan Forscher and colleagues provide an overview of music pedagogy in the middle ages and the Renaissance including the history of solfège in their book *Music Education in the Middle Ages and the Renaissance.*
5. Aurelie Barbuscia gives a history of the metronome in her article "Musical Practice Halfway between Art and Mechanics."
6. From personal experience, we find that millennials aren't always conversant with technology. There is additional evidence that the view of millennials being "digital natives," who innately interact with technology, is too general and that most millennials may have only a superficial knowledge of technology. See a discussion of this argument in Eunjung Oh and Thomas C. Reeves's article "Generational Differences and the Integration of Technology in Learning, Instruction, and Performance."
7. K. Anders Ericsson, along with colleagues Ralf Krampe and Clemens Tesch-Romer, published a landmark article in 1993 developing their theory of expert performance. The article "The Role of Deliberate Practice in the Acquisition of Expert Performance" studied expert violinists who were key to the development of this theory. For a more thorough exploration of developing expertise in musical performance see Jennifer Mishra's chapter "Musical Expertise" in *The Oxford Handbook of Expertise.*
8. Malcolm Gladwell argues in his book *Outliers* that many factors effect success. Some of these factors seem hidden and may be difficult to pinpoint. Gladwell uses the Beatles as an example of a music group that was able to accumulate 10,000 hours of practice before becoming famous.
9. K. Anders Ericsson has written extensively on the importance of deliberate practice in developing expertise. For an overview, see the chapter "Development of Elite Performance and Deliberate Practice: An Update from the Perspective of the Expert Performance Approach" in Janet Starkes and Ander Ericsson's book by *Expert Performance in Sports.*
10. Musician Nancy Barry and music psychologist Susan Hallam wrote a comprehensive and easy-to-understand overview of musical practice from a research perspective in the chapter "Practice" in the Richard Parncutt and Gary McPherson's book *The Science and Psychology of Music Performance.*
11. Marilyn J. Kostka, in her research study titled "Practice Expectations and Attitudes," found a disconnect between what applied teachers expected from practice and what the students reported both in terms of the amount of time practiced and strategies used.
12. Jennifer Bugos and Linda High, in their research titled "Perceived Versus Actual Practice Strategy Usage by Older Adult Novice Piano Students," found that adult piano students perceived using practice strategies more frequently than they actually did.

13. For an understandable look at the science behind learning see Peter Brown, Henry Roediger, and Mark McDaniel's book *Make It Stick* as well as Benedict Carey's book *How We Learn*. Both discuss the importance of distributing learning over time.
14. For music-specific research supporting distributed practice see the Barry and Hallam chapter cited earlier and Laura Stambaugh's research "When Repetition Isn't the Best Practice Strategy."
15. Harald Jørgensen extensively researched practice expectations among instrumental musicians. He provides an overview of practice research in his chapter "Strategies for Individual Practice."
16. A number of researchers have explored the effects of sleep on musical practice. One example is Amy Simmons's research "Distributed Practice and Procedural Memory Consolidation in Musicians' Skill Learning."
17. Orin O'Brien's quote is from one of our as yet unpublished research studies where we interviewed members of the New York Philharmonic about how they practice for premieres.
18. A number of researchers, including Christine Carter and Jessica Grahn, have demonstrated that interleaving practice improves performance. See their research "Optimizing Music Learning: Exploring How Blocked and Interleaved Practice Schedules Affect Advanced Performance."
19. English proverb found at https://en.oxforddictionaries.com/definition/a_change_is_as_good_as_a_rest.
20. The researchers Christine Carter and Jessica Grahn asked ten clarinetists to practice expositions from Stamitz Concertos in F and E*b* and two exercises from Jean-Xavier Lefèvre's *Methode de clarinette*.
21. Chunking has been a topic in psychological research since the mid-20th century and has been demonstrated in countless research studies. Books such as Joshua Foer's *Moonwalking with Einstein* provide down-to-earth examples of cognitive concepts such as chunking.
22. In a music-specific example, Pamela Pike and Rebecca Carter demonstrated that sight reading improved when preceded by melodic and rhythmic pattern drills. They reported their research findings in an article titled "Employing Cognitive Chunking Techniques to Enhance Sight-Reading Performance of Undergraduate Group-Piano Students."
23. William Chase and Hebert Simon showed the differences in pattern memory between expert and novice chess players in their 1973 article "Perception in Chess," and Daniel Levitin explores this phenomenon in music in the chapter "What Makes a Musician?" in his book *This Is Your Brain on Music*.
24. See Rebecca Payne Shockley's book *Mapping Music*.
25. Visit Joy Morin's website *Color in My Piano* to see the color version of this example: http://colorinmypiano.com/2015/05/01/music-mapping-with-piano-students. The notation for the piece "A Quiet Lagoon" may be found in the book *Alfred's Premier Piano Course Technique 2B* by Dennis Alexander, Gayle Kowalchyk, E. L. Lancaster, Victoria McArthur, and Martha Mier.
26. Psychologist Roger Chaffin and pianist Gabriela Imreh teamed up to research how an expert pianist learned a piece of music from sight reading to memorized performance. They coauthored a number of studies detailing their findings. One finding is what type of musical decisions a performer makes (e.g., basic decisions such as fingerings, interpretative decisions like phrasing, performance decisions like emotional expressiveness) and when these decisions are made. They detail findings in their book *Practicing Perfection*.
27. Eric Bartlett's quote is from one of our as yet unpublished research studies where we interviewed members of the New York Philharmonic about how they practice for premieres.
28. When interviewing eighth-grade instrumentalists about which practice strategies they used, Debbie Rohwer and Jeremy Polk found that many students could only name repetition as a practice strategy, but even students who did know about other practice strategies didn't use them in practicing. Their findings are published in the article "Practice Behaviors of 8th Grade Instrumental Musicians."
29. By studying how pianist Gabriela Imreh learned a piece of music, she and psychologist Roger Chaffin identified four stages of practice: a scouting-it-out stage where the musician sight reads and generally gets to know the music; a section-by-section phase where the musician works intensively on difficult sections; a putting-it-together phase where the whole piece is put back together; and a polishing stage, which is preparatory to performance. Findings are detailed in the article "Learning *Clair de Lune*: Retrieval Practice and Expert Memorization."

30. Janice Deakin described a study that she and her colleagues conducted with ice skaters. Young ice skaters were more likely to practice comfortable skills even if they intended to practice more difficult skills. The research is published in a chapter "An Examination of the Practice Environments in Figure Skating and Volleyball: A Search for Deliberate Practice" in the book *Expert Performance in Sports.*
31. Aaron Williamon and Elizabeth Valentine observed pianists learning a piece by J. S. Bach. The pianists tended to stop and start more frequently on sections that they identified as difficult as well as starting and stopping at phrase boundaries; the more difficult the section, the smaller the practice segment. Practice segments systematically lengthened as practiced progressed. See their full report in the article "The Role of Retrieval Structures in Memorizing Music."
32. See the Chaffin and Imreh book *Practicing Perfection*, detailing how an expert musician practices.
33. A number of researchers have identified the metronome as one of the most advocated and used practice strategies, including Nancy Barry and Victoria McArthur in their research article "Teaching Practice Strategies in the Music Studio."
34. Arlen Fast's quote is from an interview with Jennifer Mishra and Barbara Fast about how he practices for premieres. The full research report is the article "Practising in the New World."
35. For an overview of how visualization is used in sports, see the chapter "Visualization and Self-Hypnosis" in Costas Karageorghis and Peter Terry's book *Inside Sport Psychology.*
36. Readers interested in the brain structures involved in learning and performing music can find an overview of research in Gottfried Schlaug's chapter "Music, Musicians, and Brain Plasticity" in the *Oxford Handbook of Music Psychology*, edited by Susan Hallam and colleagues.
37. See the Barry and Hallam chapter "Practice" in Richard Parncutt and Gary McPherson's book *The Science and Psychology of Music Performance*, as well as Nancy Barry's 2007 research study "A Qualitative Study of Applied Music Lessons and Subsequent Student Practice Sessions."

2

Overlooked and Evolving Technology

Introduction

Let's start with the technology we already have in hand—literally. We're talking about cell phones, laptops, and other devices that are common in our everyday lives. The usefulness of these devices in our musical practice can be easily overlooked. Just because a technology is familiar doesn't mean we've tapped all of its potential for practicing.

This chapter is titled "Overlooked and Evolving Technology," but it could easily have been titled "Why haven't I thought of this before?!"

Musicians sometimes have a mental block, thinking that technology can only be used in one way. The term psychologists use for this type of thinking is "functional fixedness."[1] In this chapter we're going to think laterally about technology: creating practice solutions that are outside the box—or at least peaking over the top.

Metronomes don't just tick anymore

At the writing of this chapter, there are literally hundreds of different metronome apps available. Some are intuitive, others are more complex. With the new apps come new practice strategies and pedagogical interventions that would not have been possible with the original metronome. Teachers who have previously avoided metronomes may wish to revisit this evolving technology, as newer apps may be more attractive. For a historical perspective on the use of metronome as a practice strategy, see Box 2.2.

Count, click, tick, beep

Gone are the days when metronomes only ticked. The sounds created by modern metronome apps are limited only by the imagination of their developers. Instrument timbres

BOX 2.1 Visit the companion website

See the companion website 2.1 for a review of some of our favorite metronome apps.

BOX 2.2 From a historical perspective

So common is the metronome that we forget it is actually a technology not always accepted by musicians. While the metronome was invented two hundred years ago,[2] it has recently begun to evolve again with the app explosion of the 21st century.

The original—and continuing—purpose of the metronome was to help composers, like Beethoven, communicate precise tempos with the performer. It wasn't a practice tool at this point. But within ten years of its invention the metronome would be a common tool in a musician's toolkit, supported by the likes of Clementi, Kreutzer, Spohr, and Hummel.

One of the very early benefits of using the metronome was to help beginning musicians learn the correct "feel" of the beat. But from the start, musicians were wary of overuse. Then, as today, "metronomic" was synonymous with "unmusical" or "mechanical." As mentioned in chapter 1, teachers have differing philosophies about metronome use.

But as the century progressed, the tool found its place as a musical practice strategy. We don't know exactly who first thought to use the metronome as a practice tool, but one of the earliest reference in print is F. C. Meyer's "New Treatise on the Art of Playing upon the Double Movement Harp," written around 1825—ten years after the metronome was invented.[3] In this book, Meyer provides a table of exercises for practice with a slow metronome marking and a performance metronome marking and places to indicate progress in between (see Figure 2.1). Meyer writes:

> Beginning an exercise with the number on the pendulum at which the Student can play it steadily, to ensure equality of tone, and then gradually working up the time, until it can be played, firmly and freely to the highest number which will point out the progressive improvement the Student is enabled to make, until the greatest possible degree of rapidity is accomplished (p. 29).

This 19th-century practice strategy remains strongly embedded in the practice routines of modern musicians.

Containing the numbers of the Exercises to be practised by the Metronome, upon which the Student may mark the progressive improvement made in the rapidity of executing them, from the lowest to the highest number.

Ex.	Met me							Met me	Ex.	Met me							Met me
1	84. ♪							160. ♩	30	50. ♩							120. ♩
2	84. ♪							160. ♩	31	50. ♩							100. ♩
3	100. ♩							160. ♩	32	50. ♩							66. 𝅗𝅥
4	100. ♩							132. ♩	33	50. ♩							92. ♩
5	100. ♩							160. ♩	34	50. ♪							132. ♪
6	100. ♩							132. ♩	35	72. 𝅘𝅥𝅯							120. ♪
7	56. ♪							80. ♩	36	50. ♪							69. ♩
8	56. ♪							80. ♩	37	72. ♩							80. 𝅗𝅥
9	56. ♪							80. ♩	38	88. ♩							88. 𝅗𝅥
10	56. ♪							120. ♪	39	60. ♩							112. 𝅗𝅥

FIGURE 2.1 This table is one of the first examples showing the use of the metronome as a practice strategy. Students practice each exercise at a slow tempo (e.g., eighth note equals 84) and mark their progress toward the final performance goal (quarter note equals 160). This shows a practice strategy similar to how we use the metronome today, slowly increasing the tempo. Published in Meyer's harp treatise around 1825.

such as claves, cowbells, and gongs are common, as are sound effects like electronic beeps. Added to the choices are spoken numbers—in various languages—and fun sounds like a robot counting that can be motivational for young children. Some metronome apps even allow for the addition of customized sounds.[4] These sounds change up the "boring" metronome—after all, students will be practicing with these repeated sound for hours—so make it a sound they like!

Using various sounds can be fun, but these sounds can have a further usefulness in practice. Different sounds can easily be programmed on each beat or subdivision, helping students keep their place in the measure.

The silent tick: muting the beat

Sound effects are not the only addition to modern metronomes. Most add a visual beat—an idea akin to a bouncing ball placed over song lyrics in karaoke programs.[5] Some apps include a subtle visual pulse, others a full-screen color flash. Other apps also include a tactile, vibration option. Instead of an aural beat, these haptic apps provide a physical vibration on the beat. Physically feeling the pulse is particularly useful when using the metronome app on an Apple watch.[6]

Using silent flashes and vibrations gives the students the basic beat without competing with the music. This changes students' focus from listening to the beat to listening to the music.

Muting some beats in a sequence is another practice option offered on modern metronome apps. This forces students to internalize the pulse. A few metronome apps even randomly mute beats or measures, which really keeps students on their toes![7] Students can quickly discover if they are rushing or dragging the tempo. Lengthening the muted section from one beat to an entire phrase reveals stability of the internal pulse and helps students reduce dependence on the metronome prior to performance.

A tick of your own: tap-in-tempo

A feature that has been added to many metronome apps (e.g., Time Guru, Tempo, Polynome, Pro Metronome) is the ability to tap in a desired tempo.[8] "Tap, tap, tap," and the app immediately converts the tap into beats per minute. This avoids the slow trial-and-error method of adjusting the metronome repeatedly in order to find the desired tempo. The tap-in-tempo feature is quick and time-saving.

This tap-in feature is useful when finding the speed of a recording or when singing through (or internally hearing) a passage. When ensemble musicians practice, they must anticipate the conductor's tempo. One way of doing this is to listen to multiple recordings and tap in the speed to find the fastest and slowest possible tempos. This gives the ensemble performer realistic practice goals early in the learning process.

Tempos often change within a piece due to rubato or notated accelerandos or ritardandos. The changes are usually not expressed in beats per minute, but teachers may find it helpful to write in the various tempo changes as performance goals. Better still, a teacher can sing or play the changes at tempo and the student can find the performed tempos by tapping into a metronome app. This requires students to internalize the model tempos.

Changing ticks: accelerando and ritardando

Metronomes have transformed the way we practice, but they have two limitations that modern apps have tried to address.

First, as mentioned in chapter 1, using the metronome in practice involves systematically increasing the tempo. However, this necessitates stopping practice to change the metronome setting—breaking the flow of practice. Some modern apps have eliminated the need to stop by programming in automatic increases in tempo, thus becoming a progressive metronome.

Tempo by Frozen Ape,[9] for instance, allows musicians to specify the length of passage and how many beats per minute the tempo increases. The program will loop, gradually increasing the tempo with each repetition. So a musician practicing a 4-bar phrase could have the tempo increased by 5 beats per minute every 16 beats. This helps the musician stay in practice flow and not get bogged down at any one tempo.

This strategy is particularly useful when a performer reaches a tempo plateau, a point at which they cannot play the passage any faster. In these situations, it may be better to program in a systematic increase—or leap—in tempo that forces the student closer to performance tempo with each repetition, *even if notes have to be skipped to keep pace with the metronome.* This strategy can sometimes break through a practice plateau. Surprisingly, students often can actually play the passage faster than they thought.

Even after the piece can be performed at tempo, it is frequently necessary to review the foundational technique of the passage by playing it slowly. Some metronome apps will allow the performer to program in a fast-slow-fast as well as a slow-to-fast pattern. This can be a very quick review method.

One option we have not yet seen in a metronome app is the ability to select random tempos from a defined range. This is a great way to test technically difficult passages. Performance situations sometimes result in unexpected tempos. These can be due to nerves, but also in response to audience reactions and spontaneous interpretive decisions. This feature would help a musician prepare for the reality of performance.

The second problem with metronomes is that they are inflexible and don't work well with music that includes a lot of rubato or frequent tempo changes (e.g., accelerandos and ritardandos). When practicing with a metronome, musicians must either disregard the tempo change in the music or disregard the metronome. There are now a few metronome apps that allow tempo fluctuations to be programmed by the musician (e.g., Tempo Advance, Accelerando Metronome).[10]

In the Accelerando Metronome app (see Figure 2.2), the starting and ending tempos of a passage are defined as well as the number of beats within the tempo change. The app will do the math and compute a gradual accelerando or ritardando over the time frame. A musician can now practice an accelerando over 8 measures starting at 60 beats per

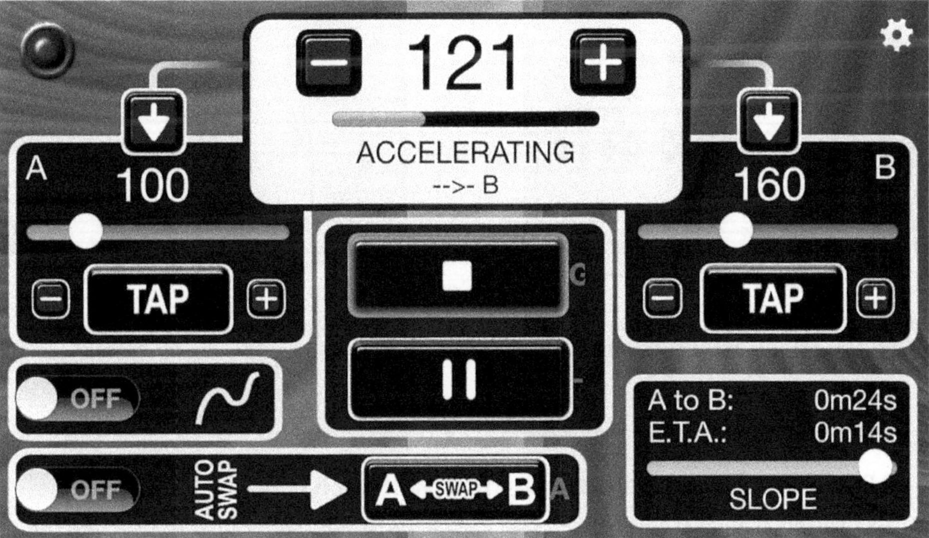

FIGURE 2.2 Screenshot of the Accelerando Metronome app in use, showing the tempo increasing from 100 to 160 over twenty-four seconds (slope). The screenshot was taken at 121 bpm with an E.T.A. to performance tempo of fourteen seconds. Clicking the A–B swap button will reverse the accelerando to a ritardando.

minute and ending at 150. With certain music, this type of app is the right tool for the job. No longer do students need to ignore or turn off the metronome when the tempo varies!

Metronomes with changing tempo features are still rare and ripe for future app designers.

Mixed ticks: compound meters and polyrhythms

With basic metronomes, practicing mixed and changing meter was impossible. The only option was to set a metronome to the smallest subdivision (e.g., the eighth note). However, there usually is a limit to how fast this subdivision can be set, and metric accents are not represented in the metronome tick.

For instance, Bartok's *Mikrokosmos* includes excellent examples of repertoire that specifically focus on complex meters. Figure 2.3 shows an excerpt of #126 of Volume 5 where Bartok didn't have a choice but to mark the eighth note at 250 beats per minute to represent a consistent pulse between metric changes. This metronome marking exceeded the upper limits of the metronomes of the time. However, even with modern metronomes, it's hard to match a subdivision at this tempo.

Advanced metronomes of the 20th century like Dr. Beat began to address more complex meters by allowing for compound meters such as 7/8. They did this by allowing the performer more choice in the number of beats per bar and the ability to choose which beats were accented. The ability to program compound meters has become a feature of some modern metronome apps.

Today, the most advanced apps like Polynome allow for almost unlimited metric variations as well as polyrhythms.[11] Polynome also allows tempo changes between

FIGURE 2.3 Notation for measures 1–6 of Bartok's *Mikrokosmos* Volume 5 #126, showing mixed and changing meter with a metronome marking of eighth note equals 250.

BOX 2.3 Visit the companion website

Visit the companion website 2.2 to view a video tutorial on how to program the Time Guru Metronome app for the mixed and changing meter of the first 6 measures of Bartok's *Mikrokosmos* Volume 5 #126.

measures to be programmed. This is still a rare feature in metronome apps. In chapter 4, we'll discuss another way to create unique click tracks that have unlimited variability in tempo and meter.

Slowdowners: metronome variation

Slowdowner apps can function much like metronomes, allowing tempos to speed up and slow down, but unlike metronomes, there is no external beat.

In apps such as the Amazing Slow Downer,[12] an mp3 file is uploaded into the app. From there, the tempo of the recording can be changed without modulating the pitch. This allows the performer to play along with the music at faster or slower speeds. Performers can isolate difficult passages and use the strategy of slow-to-fast practice, just like using a metronome. The passages can even be looped for seamless repeated practicing. We'll discuss these apps in more detail in chapter 3 when we focus on practicing with recordings.

Seeing sound: tuners in the 21st century

Throughout history, musicians have found a way of using technology to help with developing fundamentals—metronomes to develop pulse, and tuners to develop intonation. Like metronomes, tuners are now widely available as apps.

Most tuner apps simulate features found on physical chromatic tuners by visually representing intonation and providing visual feedback to performers. These apps vary by range and sensitivity, and many allow for various tuning temperaments. Apps may also include tone generators that can be adjusted by frequency (e.g., A = 440 or A = 445) and timbre.

App designers have begun exploring novel ways of visually representing sound and providing feedback to the musician. Sound can be shown in the form of waves, dials, pitch names, and frequencies, and now performers can choose the type of interface they prefer. Feedback options such as colors or icons (e.g., smiley faces) provide information and motivation. Many apps include multiple sound representations on one screen, which allows for very fine tuning of the pitch. Tunable,[13] for instance, includes the pitch name and octave, hertz, cent deviation, a sine wave that moves across the screen to show pitch deviation, and a color spectrum to indicate whether the pitch is acceptably in tune (green)—all on one screen (see Figure 2.4).

BOX 2.4 Visit the companion website

Visit the companion website 2.3 for reviews of some of our favorite tuner apps.

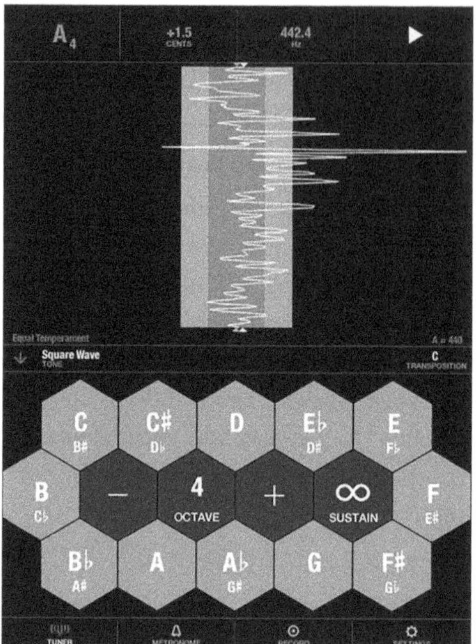

FIGURE 2.4 Screenshot of the app Tuneable taken by Courtney Mantle, showing the various ways the app provides intonation feedback (e.g., pitch name, hertz, cents, sine wave, color).

Tuning apps often include a tone generator to produce a reference pitch for tuning instruments. These, as well as specific apps such as Drone Tone Tool,[14] can be used to create drones as a reference pitch to develop correct intonation. Playing against a drone helps to develop correct intonation, particularly within a chord.

Pitch history is a feature starting to be included in tuning apps like Tunable,[15] which tracks general tuning tendencies. Students can see if they are moving closer to reference pitches over time. Tuners like iStroboSoft even have noise filters that focus on one performer in the middle of an ensemble.[16] Some apps have been developed with specific instruments in mind, like guitar, but most tuners can be useful for all musicians to develop their inner ear.

The main advantage of a tuner app is accessibility. Rather than purchasing a separate dedicated tuner, this function can be bundled with other features into one app (for instance, a metronome, tuner, and recording device). One drawback to using a tuner is reliance on the visual feedback. Advanced tuning apps like TonalEnergy address this issue by allowing students to record a passage into the app (without looking!) and then playing the recording back to see how in tune they were.[17] This app even allows the performer to play along with a recording (their own, or a reference recording), isolating the student's pitch from the recorded pitch.

Wikipedia and the web

The World Wide Web is now central to our lives. We use it to socialize, to find information, and for entertainment. Phones and computers are in everyone's hands these days, and the amount of instant access to information on the web is astounding. "Google" is now a verb—it's something we do when we need information quickly.

Some teachers have embraced the web as a place to get information and find pedagogical ideas. However, teachers don't always think to integrate the web into music lessons. Some websites are absolute gems, with well-designed, informative, and motivational multimedia resources that teachers can use to enhance lessons. The question is not *if* valuable resources exist on the Internet; the question is how to find appropriate websites amidst those of little educational value.

In this section, we'll introduce a few of our favorite websites and give some tips in finding those web gems that are useful in the music classroom and studio. The three main types of websites we'll discuss are 1) informational, 2) digital score resources, and 3) interactive websites.

Curiosity doesn't actually kill cats

Technology has made information accessible, but accessibility doesn't necessarily breed curiosity. Students now can find out almost anything about everything. However, teachers may need to encourage this curiosity and guide students toward important and interesting information about the pieces they are studying.

This information helps bring the music to life and can be stylistically useful, informing performance decisions. If students find the information for themselves, they will likely remember it and be more invested in the information. The teacher's role is to guide students toward key concepts. A teacher may need to continually prompt students by asking questions. It's important for the students to find the information for themselves. But remember, just because information is online, doesn't make it true. Be sure to have the conversation with students about cross-checking their information.

Finding information is more fun if it is presented as a treasure hunt game. In a class or group situation, students can crowdsource the information, each tossing an interesting fact into the conversation. This can become a bit competitive, but in a fun way! For instance, when studying one of Brahms's *Hungarian Dances*, students can look up interesting information on Brahms himself and details specific to the piece.

Word cloud apps like Wordle (also known as "tag clouds") transform text into fun and colorful art.[18] Suddenly, rather boring facts become more interesting—and hopefully easier to remember—if presented visually (see Figure 2.5).

For pieces that are taught frequently, teachers can share word clouds made by other students and compare and contrast words that were included or omitted.

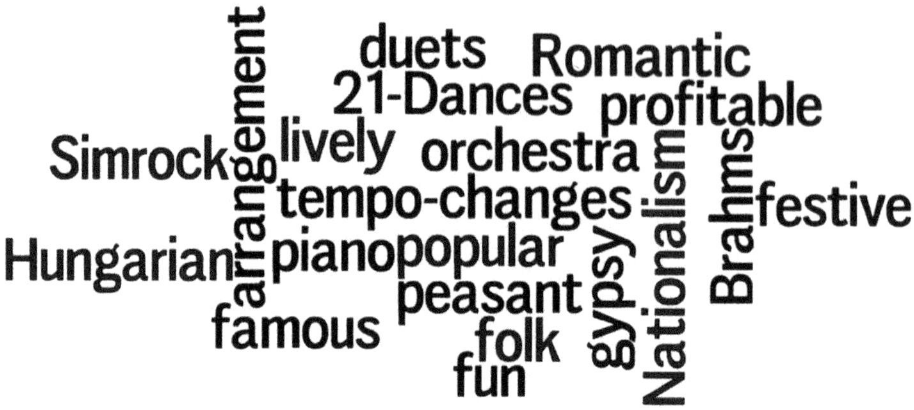

FIGURE 2.5 Word cloud based on facts about Brahms's *Hungarian Dances* created using the app Wordle.

With all this information collected, it is now easy for students to talk about their pieces at a recital, and the word cloud can provide the basis for writing program notes.

Music at your fingertips: IMSLP and other digital sources

Information about music isn't the only thing that we can find online. The music itself is now often available.

For example, musicians can access digital copies of public domain music from the International Music Score Library Project (IMSLP).[19] All sorts of music can be downloaded: solo, chamber, ensemble scores, and parts. Recently, IMSLP added downloadable recordings. IMSLP provides copyright information to help musicians determine whether a piece is available as public domain in their country.

The historical editions found on IMSLP can be particularly useful. These show how the composer originally notated a piece or how various editors interpreted the music. Studying these historical editions may bring new insights to a performance. The New York Philharmonic has also made their digital archive available.[20] The scores and parts include bowings and fingerings used in performance and the conductors' scores indicate musical decisions. For instance, the scores of Beethoven's *Symphony No. 7* contain markings by Mahler, Toscanini, and Bernstein.

Also available online, publishers and distributors like J. W. Pepper and Luck's Music Library are making purchased music available for download.[21] Additionally, several contemporary composers (e.g., pianist Greg Anderson of the piano duo Anderson & Roe, and Jennifer Higdon) are electing to self-publish directly from their websites.[22] Amateur composers can even self-publish compositions on J. W. Pepper or directly, through notation programs such as Sibelius and MuseScore.[23] These resources are also useful for teachers who want to share their own unique exercises.

The field of music publishing is an evolving landscape, with young musicians often using a combination of print and digital scores. We'll return to this topic later in this chapter when we discuss using digital files in a concert setting. Teachers are key in helping students find quality music regardless of the source.

And now for the games!: interactive websites

The web is more than a static textbook—it moves!

Interactive websites have the feel of a game, but with content music teachers value. These websites range from simple quizzes to powerful pedagogical tools. If designed well, interactive websites motivate students to learn and spend more time with the material.

Three of the factors we looked for when choosing websites and apps for this chapter were ease-of-use, educational value, and stability. We chose websites that were almost instantly usable. Not only do students have a limited attention span—so do we! The goal is to teach the music through the website rather than teaching how to use the website. Another factor in our choice was the depth of educational value of the website. The following websites have broad ranging applications for music instruction. We also chose websites that have stability. The benefit of the web is that it's always changing—and the downside is that it's always changing. Major educational organizations, such as PBS and the BBC, and some symphony orchestras, like the Dallas Symphony, New York Philharmonic, and San Francisco Symphony, frequently develop and update their online educational content.

We've chosen a few well-designed and pedagogically rich websites to share in this section that will enhance music practice. We save our discussion of online music notation programs for chapter 4, and YouTube will have a key place in chapter 3 when we explore the use of recordings.

The Sight Reading Factory, released in 2011 (see Figure 2.6), generates unlimited sight reading examples.[24] The program allows for extensive customization of the exercises

FIGURE 2.6 Screenshot of a level 2 string ensemble sight reading exercise created by Sight Reading Factory. The parameters were to generate four string parts with a random key signature and meter.

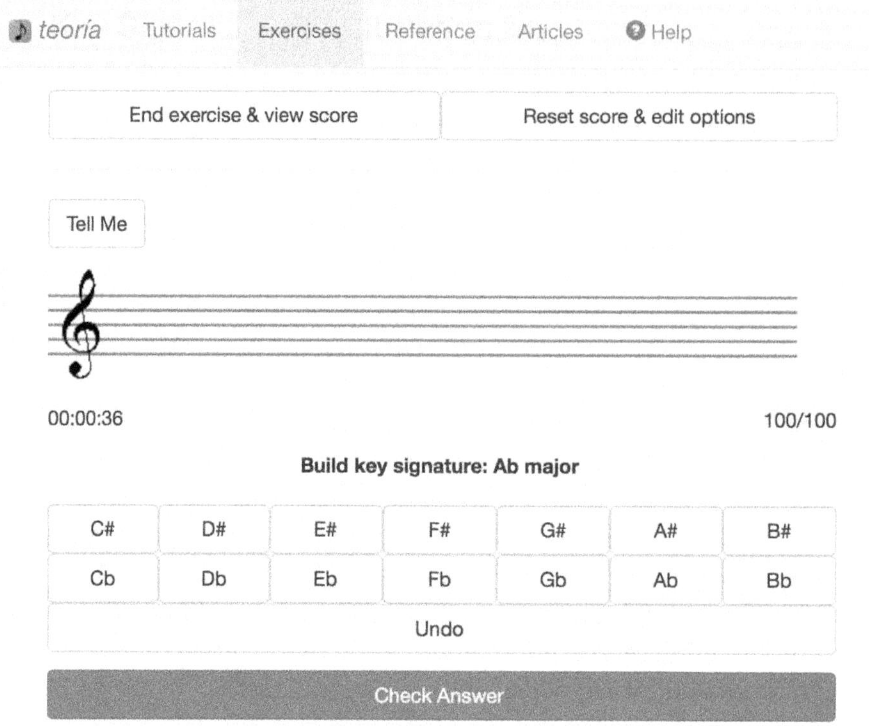

FIGURE 2.7 Screenshot of the Teoria website for the exercise "Key Signature Construction." Students build key signatures by clicking on the appropriate flat or sharp, in this case for the key of A♭ major.

(difficulty, tempo, length, key, meter, preview time, etc.). Examples can be generated for solo instruments, including piano and voice, or ensembles of various instrumentation, either unison or multipart. Solfège can be included in the exercises. The students can even generate new exercises to sight read at home. They can then record their sight reading and send to the teacher for evaluation. The program is relatively inexpensive for the teacher with subscription costs varying by class or studio size.

Teoria is an example of a powerful music theory tutorial program that has been online since 1998 (though it has changed significantly over the years).[25] This program includes theory lessons and customizable exercises, both written and ear training. Exercises include everything from basic note reading to advanced transposition and extended jazz chords (see Figure 2.7). The teacher can adjust difficulty level, so this program can work with students of varying abilities and instrumentation. The app is free, but with a subscription, students can save their scores for grading purposes. An alternative program to Teoria is musictheory.net (Tenuto is the app version of this program).[26] This program has similar features, though exercises may not be as advanced as Teoria.

SmartMusic is both an assessment tool and a virtual accompanist.[27] Currently it is most frequently used in school ensemble programs, but may also be useful in studio settings. The program contains an extensive library that includes most method books, published solos, and music for large ensemble.

Teachers can customize how the program evaluates students, deciding on length of assignment, tempo, and whether or not students can see their errors. Students play into the computer's microphone and the program grades their performances. If feedback is turned on, students will immediately see their rhythmic and pitch errors and scores are sent directly to the teacher's grade book (see Figure 2.8).

The program will also accompany students on solos or allow them to hear their part in the ensemble. Some states, such as Illinois and New York, allow students to use SmartMusic accompaniment at competitions.

The program is subscription-based, but there is a free version for teachers who would like to create their own content. Currently the program only assesses one line of music, which limits usefulness for pianists. However, Piano Maestro includes many of the assessment features of SmartMusic and is designed specifically for young children.[28]

These are just a few examples of interactive music websites. The web is dynamic—it keeps evolving. As designers become more creative with the online interface, these types of websites will only increase. The challenge for music teachers is to find resources that are both motivating and educationally valuable.

FIGURE 2.8 Screenshot of SmartMusic, showing how the program graded an excerpt. The light gray notes are incorrectly performed in this excerpt of *A Chesapeake Bay Adventure* by Vince Gassi. These would show in color within the program to indicate melodic and rhythmic errors. Use by permission of SmartMusic®.

> ### BOX 2.5 Visit the companion website
>
> See the companion website 2.4 for reviews of some useful interactive websites as well as annotation programs.

The imitation game: copiers, scanners, and PDFs

In this section, we will talk about copying music—not copying en masse to avoid copyright, but isolated copying to enhance practicing in various ways. Copies allow flexibility: we are freer to manipulate copies, cutting them apart and coloring them up, in ways we would never think to do with an original part.

While most of the strategies we'll describe use copies as part of the learning process, it should be noted that performance would usually still take place from the original score.

We'll talk both about low-tech and high-tech copies. By "low-tech" we mean photocopying. Yes, photocopiers! Photocopiers are an example of technology that is not always fully utilized in the 21st-century music practice room. For instance, simply enlarging musical notation makes it easier to read with fewer errors. Even young students can struggle with small notation, and as we age the problem is exacerbated. Musicians can benefit from enlarging fast passagework, especially containing lots of accidentals, or music containing ornaments. This strategy is also very useful when reading handwritten parts, which are not always easy to read.

By "high-tech" we're referring to digital music that is available on computers or tablets. Digital annotations can be much more dynamic, using specially created music annotation apps as well as basic PDF (portable document format) readers.

We'll talk about using both low-tech and high-tech music copies pedagogically during the practice process, but we'll also discuss the new trend of using digital scores in performance. Let's start with annotating scores during practice.

The art of annotation

Marking important information into a score is an important practice strategy. As mentioned in chapter 1, there are many things that can be marked into a part. These include fingerings, rhythms, phrase markings, form, articulations, rubato, dynamics, self-comments, and practice goals, among other things.

Teachers have varying philosophies about how much or how little students should mark in their music, but writing in at least some reminders helps to solidify the learning. One option is to start with writing in lots of markings and then gradually removing them as they are internalized. Alternatively, teachers may prefer that students write in only the most essential markings.

The important thing is to make solid performance decisions early. Marking these into the score encourages consistent technical practice. When choices aren't made, for instance when two or three possible fingerings exist, they can create disastrous conflict or hesitations in performance (i.e., performance errors). But remember, things change and it's okay to revise markings in the part as decisions evolve. The way markings are added and removed in the part can be a central part of the learning process.

There is a low-tech and a high-tech way of marking parts. We'll start with the low-tech, photocopying option.

Low-tech annotations

Making photocopies of purchased music opens up pedagogical opportunities to mark up the score. Teachers generally advocate using pencil, making it easy to change or remove markings. Photocopies allow performers to go beyond the pencil and dramatically mark up a score in ways that would be unthinkable if working with the original part.

Some students respond strongly to color. Marking photocopies with different colored pencils, highlighters, or inks to represent various musical elements (e.g., fingerings in red, dynamics in green) helps students focus on important elements. Highlighting similarities and differences (form) with color can help students understand the music at a deeper level and organize their practice. At a glance, students can immediately see the repetitions. Figure 2.9 was created by Daniel Jacobson, in which he highlights in color the fugal entrances of Bach's Fugue in C minor from *The Well-Tempered Clavier*, Book 1. He also writes in his personal understanding of the form of the piece using brackets as well as short written phrases.

Taking this a step further, photocopied scores provide the opportunity for teachers and students to liberally mark up the music with personal comments or experimental ideas. Markings highlight whatever is important in the moment, including passages that

FIGURE 2.9 Score of Bach's *The Well-Tempered Clavier*, book 1, Fugue in C minor, annotated by Daniel Jacobson. Original annotation uses color to show voicing (CS1, CS2, SUB).

need intensive practice. Everything can be included, since these are temporary and continually evolving parts. Later, important markings can be transferred into the original score once learning is established and decisions have been stabilized. Douglas Niedt, a guitar teacher based at the University of Missouri–Kansas City Conservatory, utilizes this idea extensively in his applied studio. Box 2.7 is a quote, and Figure 2.10 is an example of a working part from his website.[29]

Obviously, Figure 2.10 is a working copy; it would be virtually impossible to perform from this version. In this case, it becomes just as important to remove markings, choosing the key decisions to transfer into the original part or a fresh photocopy. This requires students to think carefully about what markings are essential to performance. Everything else may have been important during the learning process, but now it's only clutter.

Don't throw these copies away! They can be useful when revisiting a piece, documenting the process of making key decisions.

So far, we've been talking about adding and then removing markings throughout the learning process. Another approach is to start students with an absolutely clean photocopy—whiting out all editorial markings including tempo, phrase markings, dynamics, or style markings. From there, the student (with the teacher's guidance) makes all musical decisions to create a meaningful performance. This empowers the students as independent musicians and creates a sense of ownership. They develop a deeper understanding into the decision-making process usually done by editors, teachers, and composers.[30]

BOX 2.6 Visit the companion website

See companion website 2.5 for the full-color annotations of Bach's *Fugue in C minor* from *The Well-Tempered Clavier*, book 1, created by Daniel Jacobson.

BOX 2.7 From a teacher and performer

When a new student comes for their first lesson, I ask them to bring copies of the music they are working on. I specify that I want to see their "working copies" of the music, not a new, pristine copy. I can easily tell a lot about how the student practices by viewing the working copy. If it is full of markings, fingerings, circled measures, comments, notes, etc., I know they have a good understanding of how to practice and learn a piece. If the working copy is fairly clean with very few markings, I know we will have a lot of work to do on how to learn and practice a piece.

—Douglas Niedt, guitarist

FIGURE 2.10 An excerpt from Bach's *Prelude, Fugue, and Allegro* marked by guitarist Douglas Niedt. In the original score, colored pencils are used for different markings.

> **BOX 2.8 Visit the companion website**
>
> See companion website 2.6 for the full-color markings of Bach's *Prelude, Fugue, and Allegro* by guitarist Douglas Niedt.

High-tech annotations

Annotating digital PDFs is like marking photocopied music on steroids. Adding fingerings and other symbols is quick, and keeps scores tidy and easy-to-read. Markings in digital programs look more like published editorial markings, adding a sense of importance in comparison to a hand-marked score.

There are a number of apps specially designed for reading and annotating musical scores (e.g., forScore, Piascore).[31] Publishers such as Henle have also created their own annotation app.[32] The annotation features included in these programs are easy to use and allow almost unlimited customization of the music. In reality, any program or app that allows writing on PDFs will work to annotate musical notation. The Preview app built into the ios system and Adobe Reader being the most common.[33] Many of the current note-taking apps useful on mobile devices (e.g., Notability, Evernote) also include simple annotation features for PDFs.[34]

Figure 2.11 shows markings in a euphonium part in a wind ensemble piece using the forScore app. The forScore program allows for both hand drawn markings and

BOX 2.9 Visit the companion website

See the companion website 2.7 for a video tutorial on annotating music using Preview.

FIGURE 2.11 An excerpt from a euphonium part from *Concerto for Euphonium and Wind Ensemble*, III, by Eric Ewazen, marked in forScore by Eli Breon.

inserted symbols (for instance, the tonguing mark "T"), which look very much like a professional edits.

Sharing music, with or without annotations, is easy in most programs. Teachers can make their own personal annotated score to share with students to get them started on a piece. Throughout the week, students can continue to share annotations with their teacher or even other students. This is particularly useful if the teacher gives an assignment, such as solidify fingerings in a passage, with a deadline due before the next lesson. This is one way to make sure the students are meeting practice goals and it allows the teacher to provide immediate feedback with annotated comments.

The layering feature on many annotation apps allows musical decision history to be saved. During the course of practice, thoughts on fingerings, breathing, and interpretations change. Rather than erasing the original markings, create a new layer for new decisions. The initial version isn't deleted; it's just hidden, so the musician can always return to earlier annotations for reference.

As we discussed with low-tech photocopies, removing markings as performance approaches is just as important as adding them to the music. Using layers is similar to making multiple photocopies. Each layer includes different annotations representing different stages of the learning process. It is easy to switch layers on and off to hide or reveal more or fewer annotations.

Another way students can layer is by musical element, for instance by marking dynamics on a different layer from articulations. This, combined with the color-coding options of most annotation apps, really highlights the diverse musical elements. Teachers can use the musical elements to drive practice goals, one week focusing on dynamics, another week focusing on articulations.

Some digital programs also allow for white annotations (using a white pen or box), which blocks out features of the score such as notes or measures. This feature may be particularly helpful to temporarily block out distracting elements such as ornaments or passing tones. For instance, having students play only the notes on the beat is made easier if the other notes are simply removed from the score. These can be added back in (the white annotations removed) when the student is ready. This digital whiteout feature is also particularly useful during the memorization process. Notes or measures can be temporarily blocked out to check memory.

Many music annotation programs include multiple features such as metronomes, tuners, online keyboards, and recording devices. We'll talk more about how to pedagogically utilize the recording features in chapter 3.

Cutting it apart

We would never consider physically cutting up an original score, but it's no problem to cut apart a photocopy or a digital PDF. There are several powerful pedagogical benefits to being able to cut the music into parts.

Practice puzzle

Music teachers often use flash cards for learning notes or terminology, but this same strategy can work for practicing music. Difficult passages can be cut into small chunks, either physically or digitally, and isolated onto flash cards. These flash cards can be shuffled, setting up a random test of learning (see Figure 2.12). Even the experts benefit from this type of interleaving activity.

FIGURE 2.12 Illustration of flash cards created for first phrase of Giovanni Battista Martini's *Gavotte* for violin and piano.

In Box 2.10, Sherry Sylar describes a playful way of interleaving practice—focusing attention on a difficult section and being able to jump into the middle of a piece, literally at random. As mentioned in chapter 1, interleaving practice is returning to a piece or a section of a piece repeatedly throughout one practice session. Flash cards will naturally create interleaving practice since passages will return at random times—making practice a game. This flash card activity also works well when memorizing music.

An easy way to create high-tech versions of interleaving flash cards is to use slideshow apps like the one included in iPhoto.[36] First, take a screenshot, photo, or scan of the challenging passages to create the flash cards.[37] Then, send the resulting photos or PDFs directly to the camera roll of a mobile device. Most slideshow apps will randomize the presentation of the flash cards, creating made-to-order interleaving practice.

Rather than creating flash cards, teachers may prefer to place challenging passages on a single page creating a "hard part practice sheet" (see Figure 2.13). Students can see all the difficult passages that need practicing at a glance. This encourages students to interleave practicing and quickly return to difficult sections without being distracted by page turns and the easier music in between. When creating a hard part practice sheet, the passages do not necessarily need to be ordered as they occur in the music. Teachers can order the passages from easiest to most difficult (or visa versa), or place like passages together.

BOX 2.10 From a performer

I made flash cards for the Berio Sequenza so that I wouldn't make the mistake of practicing from the beginning to measure 32 and say, "oh, shoot, I'd better go over that again," practicing the first 32 bars way too much and not practicing the last 32 bars enough. I actually enlarged the music and excerpted the phrases or sections relevant to special practice needs, printing them on cards and numbering them. I divided the piece up in phrases. Not only were there especially difficult small sections, but there were also sections that included carryovers, musical transitions, that I was intent on being able to communicate. I think there were about fifteen "flash cards" for the Sequenza, and I would shuffle them up or sometimes I would say randomly, "okay, number 13," and I would pull out my 13 music and play it.

—Sherry Sylar, oboist, New York Philharmonic[35]

BOX 2.11 Visit the companion website

Visit the companion website 2.8 and 2.9 to view tutorials on how to make digital flash cards using Preview and iPhoto slideshow feature.

"UNFINISHED" SYMPHONY

No. 8—B minor

Viola

Franz Schubert (Oct. 30, 1822)

Allegro moderato

FIGURE 2.13 A digital hard part practice sheet created for the viola part of Schubert *Symphony No.* 8 in b minor. Music was first scanned using TurboScan, and Preview was used to excerpt the challenging sections for practice.

Memory jogger

Similar to a practice sheet, are memory cue sheets. A memory cue sheet is the entire piece boiled down to a handful of musical reminders, pasted or digitally represented on one (or at the most two) pages. It's important to remember that even when musicians perform with music, they aren't reading every single note.[38] A memory cue sheet is in reality a representation of how performers are likely referencing their notation during performance.

A memory cue sheet can include note cues (anything from a single chord to a few measures of a passage) or comments. These often are landmarks or "jump points" that represent important points in the music. Also important to include are transitions or "switches" where two passages are similar, but have minor changes that lead to different sections.

The cue sheet can even include—or completely consist of—a visual map. We talked about making visual maps of a piece in chapter 1. These maps visually represent the music using lines, curves, shapes, slash patterns, or whatever makes sense to the performer. The important part is that the similar passages are represented visually in similar ways. In reality, a cue sheet can include anything that makes sense to the performer and prompts memory.

These cue sheets are helpful during the learning process, but can also help with performance anxiety that often increases when performing from memory. Some students may have a piece memorized, but need the cue sheet for confidence. Teachers will need to consider whether they are comfortable with students performing from a cue sheet or not. A digital copy on a tablet or phone may be much less intrusive than a paper copy.

Digital files in the concert hall

PDFs have been around since the 1990s, but only recently with the popularity of laptops, tablets, and phones have musicians considered using these files in practice and performance. Following the trend of electronic textbooks, some music classroom teachers have moved to using digital music scores.

The ability to access large amounts of music in the form of digital files is a major advantage for musicians, allowing them to make gig books and have music available for emergency performances. Any musician who travels with large amounts of bulky music can appreciate the benefits, as big scores suddenly become very portable. Performers have peace of mind, as their music is available for practice at any time.

Apps like forScore and unrealBook have customizable cataloging functions that help musicians organize their digital libraries.[39] These apps allow musicians to make digital gig books (called a "set list" in forScore), keeping various aspects of performing life in order in one place. For instance, string quartets performing for weddings can make a collection for various aspects of the ceremony (e.g., the procession, reception) and accompanists can keep all of their music in one place.

Digital music files are not just for the professional musician. "I forgot my music" is a common refrain from music students. Digital files stored on the students' phones or tablets mean that they will always have their music available. Using an app like TurboScan, teachers can also quickly scan students' music, making a quick reference copy with all annotations to date. This particularly helps teachers with large studios keep track of student progress.

BOX 2.12 From the news

As students arrive for this year's (2017) Yorkshire Young Sinfonia (YYS) course and concert with Ray Chen, one thing will be missing . . . all the sheet music. Thanks to the music app Newzik, students will be met by a room filled with iPads. The use of digital technology instead of traditional sheet music is still new in the classical music world, with only a handful of professional orchestras trying out this innovation so far. "The use of digital technology for orchestras has been advancing in recent times, but as yet no youth orchestra has actually performed an entire concert using only screens," said conductor Tom Hammond.

—music critic Norman Lebrecht[40]

More recently, musicians are starting to perform from digital music. For instance, iPads are becoming larger for easier reading, and there are now lay-flat versions of laptops (e.g., Microsoft Surface Laptop) that can be placed on a music stand. Turning pages is now simple, with wireless or bluetooth foot pedals and apps that allow for hands-free page turning.[41]

Musicians have also discovered a couple of added benefits of reading from digital music files. The backlit screen can overcome dim performance lighting, hands-free page turning eliminates the need for a dedicated page-turner, and there is no need to fear a breeze turning over a page of music by accident.

More and more musicians are adapting to performing from digital scores (for an example see Box 2.12). The trend may be a bit slower in classical music, but already a few orchestral musicians are choosing to perform from digitized parts. Individual solo performers are also choosing to read from digital music in concert. Tablets are much less intrusive than a musical score on a piano desk, and page turning is hidden from the audience—allowing them to forget that the tablet is even there.

Conclusion

The best thing about the technology discussed in this chapter is that it is familiar. We already know—and love—our phones, tablets, and computers. Music teachers can put these common devices to work, using them in unique ways to help students learn music better and more efficiently. Both low-tech and high-tech options are available to teachers, allowing them to create innovative practice strategies.

Both teachers and performers are changing the way they approach a musical score. The trusty metronome has evolved into a new and powerful learning tool with the app explosion. The web has become an important resource for music education. The annotation features of various apps allow for new practice strategies, and musicians are beginning to perform from digital files. The resources available online are astounding, particularly access to musical parts and historical editions. These will only continue to expand as web designers find creative ways to present musical material.

In the next chapter we'll continue to talk about apps and web resources and how they can be used to encourage listening and reflection.

Notes

1. Karl Duncker coined the phrase "functional fixedness" based on his research on problem solving. He defined it as a "mental block against using an object in a new way that is required to solve a problem" in his article "On Problem-Solving."
2. Johann Maelzel (1772–1838) invented the metronome in 1815. (We all missed the metronome's 200th anniversary!) For readers interested in more of the history behind the metronome and its reception, see Alexander Bonus's chapter "Metronome" in *Oxford Handbooks Online*, www.oxfordhandbooks.com/view/10.1093/oxfordhb/9780199935321.001.0001/oxfordhb-9780199935321-e-001.
3. Frederic Charles Meyer, New Treatise on the Art of Playing Upon the Double Movement Harp.
4. Time Guru Metronome is one app that includes many different sounds including vocal counting. Teachers may want to recommend the best sounds from the list, but it is fun to play with the nontraditional sounds. See https://avibortnick.net/time-guru.
5. One program, Bounce Metronome, found at http://bouncemetronome.com/, is fun and really takes advantage of the visual motion. Any program that scrolls music in time will serve a similar function.
6. Pulse–Haptic Metronome is an example of an app that utilizes vibration technology. See https://itunes.apple.com/us/app/pulse-haptic-metronome-for-watch/id1097323003?mt=8.
7. Time Guru Metronome, for instance, is easily programmed to mute random beats from 0 to 100 percent (flashes only). The app gradually works up to the percentage chosen and this preset can be saved for future use. See https://avibortnick.net/time-guru.
8. Information about Time Guru Metronome may be found at https://avibortnick.net/time-guru. Information about Tempo may be found at www.frozenape.com/tempo-metronome.html. Information about Polynome may be found at http://polynome.net. Information about Pro Metronome may be found at http://eumlab.com/pro-metronome.
9. Information about Tempo may be found at www.frozenape.com/tempo-metronome.html.
10. Information about Tempo Advance may be found at www.frozenape.com/tempoadvance-metronome.html. Information about Aceelerando Metronome may be found at http://seanluciw.com/AccelerandoMetronomo.php.
11. Information about Polynome may be found at http://polynome.net.
12. Information about the Amazing Slow Downer may be found at https://itunes.apple.com/us/app/amazing-slow-downer/id308998718?mt=8.
13. Information about Tunable may be found at http://tunable.affinityblue.com.
14. Information about Drone Tone Tool may be found at www.dronetonetool.com.
15. Information about Tunable may be found at http://tunable.affinityblue.com.
16. Information about iStroboSoft may be found at www.petersontuners.com/products/istrobosoft.
17. Information about TonalEnergy may be found at https://play.google.com/store/apps/details?id=com.sonosaurus.tonalenergytuner&hl=en.
18. There are many easy-to-use word cloud (or tag cloud) apps, including Wordle www.wordle.net and Word Clouds www.wordclouds.com.
19. IMSLP may be accessed at http://imslp.org.
20. The New York Philharmonic digital archives may be accessed at http://archives.nyphil.org.
21. J. W. Pepper may be accessed at www.jwpepper.com. Luck's Music Library may be accessed at www.lucksmusic.com.

22. Music composed by Greg Anderson may be accessed at www.gregandersonpiano.com/scores. Jennifer Higdon's music may be found at www.jenniferhigdon.com.
23. Go to www.jwpepper.com/myscore to access J. W. Pepper's My Score page. To learn more about Sibelius, go to www.avid.com/sibelius. To search for sheet music available on MuseScore, go to https://musescore.com/sheetmusic?utm_source=handbook.
24. The URL for the Sight Reading Factory is www.sightreadingfactory.com.
25. Teoria's homepage may be found at http://teoria.com/index.php.
26. Both the online version and links to the mobile apps for MusicTheory.net may be accessed at www.musictheory.net.
27. More information about SmartMusic is available at www.smartmusic.com.
28. More information about Piano Maestro and other apps by JoyTunes may be found at www.joytunes.com/apps.
29. Read Douglas Niedt's entire blog posting about marking music at http://douglasniedt.com/markupyourmusic.html.
30. We are indebted to Suzanne Tirk at the University of Oklahoma for suggesting the idea of whiting out editorial marks in the music in her presentation "Students Teaching Students: Strategies for Creating a Culture of Excellence in the Studio and in the Classroom," presented at Oklahoma Music Teachers State Conference in 2017.
31. The forScore app may be found at https://forscore.co. The piaScore app may be found at http://piascore.com.
32. Henle annotation app may be accessed through their music library at www.henle-library.com/en.
33. For instructions on how to annotate using Adobe Reader, go to https://helpx.adobe.com/acrobat/using/commenting-pdfs.html.
34. Information on Notability may be found at http://gingerlabs.com. Evernote's website is https://evernote.com.
35. The quote from Sherry Sylar, oboist with the New York Philharmonic, is from an unpublished research study conducted by the authors titled "An Exploration of Practicing Strategies Related to the Premiere of Classical Music."
36. Other apps are available to randomize photos, such as Random Slideshow. See https://itunes.apple.com/us/app/random-slideshow/id1143559364?mt=8.
37. Turboscan is available for IOS or Android. The ios version may be found at https://itunes.apple.com/us/app/turboscan-document-receipt-scanner/id1017559099?mt=8. Quiz-making apps such as Quizlet are also useful in creating high-tech practice flash cards, though some require a premium account to make photo flash cards and not all apps have the ability to repeatedly randomize the cards.
38. Research shows that expert musicians read music in units rather than note by note. We know this because musicians make "proofreader's errors": correcting embedded mistakes in the notation to make the music sound correct. John Sloboda documented this phenomenon in his article "The Effect of Item Position on the Likelihood of Identification by Inference in Prose Reading and Music Reading."
39. The unrealBook app may be accessed at https://itunes.apple.com/us/app/unrealbook/id370135173?mt=8.
40. See the press release published by British music critic Norman Lebrecht on his classical music blog *Slipped Disc*, April 19, 2017, http://slippedisc.com/2017/04/youth-orchestra-abolishes-sheet-music.
41. AirTurn, for instance, makes various Bluetooth foot pedals compatible with many music notation apps. See https://www.airturn.com.

3

And the Ears Have It!

Listening and Self-Recording

Introduction

Today's technology allows for truly new ways to interact with our musical sound. Traditionally, using recordings has not necessarily been a go-to practice strategy,[1] primarily because of limits to the technology,[2] but with current advances this strategy is now easy to integrate into the everyday practice routine.

Both hardware (cell phones) and software (apps) have become so simple that even the youngest students can easily record themselves and—more importantly—listen to themselves play. Specialty equipment is still available for those who want higher quality recordings, but for practicing, mobile devices provide a pedagogically useful entry point.

In this chapter we'll explore practical ideas for incorporating recordings—both audio and video—into practice. We'll start from the very beginning of the learning process by creating musical expectations through aural models, including teacher-recorded models. We'll then move into the benefits of recording weekly lessons and expand into the use of daily practice recordings to facilitate student ownership of their own learning. We'll finish with a discussion of the new trend of online performances and auditions.

"If I can hear it, I can play it" is a quote from New York Philharmonic bassoonist Arlen Fast.[3] This quote sums up the importance of integrating recordings and listening into practicing. Music is a sound art, but many student musicians underestimate the value of listening to the music they are practicing.

Modeling magic: creating musical expectations

Teachers often model for students. It's often quicker to show students how to do something than to explain a technique. Recordings, both professional recordings and teacher-recorded models, allow students to hear the entire piece (and all the parts) before they can physically perform the music. Research shows that practice is more effective when students listen to appropriate musical examples.[4]

Teachers' views vary on how much students should listen to teacher models and recordings. Some believe that listening is an essential component to learning music, a view embodied in pedagogies such as Suzuki.[5] Other teachers believe that students need to develop their own, independent interpretations without reference to aural models. Many teachers embrace a position somewhere in between, believing that some listening is beneficial, especially if the student listens to multiple models.

With the advent of YouTube in 2005, a new era of recording access opened up. Multiple performances of all levels are now easily available to students.[6] There are websites and browser plug-ins that allow recordings to be downloaded from YouTube,[7] though there may be copyright considerations. Teachers may wish to download recordings to ensure they remain available for future use.

In this section we'll discuss using technology to enhance teacher modeling and how to effectively find and use recordings, including those available on YouTube. We'll introduce practice strategies that emphasize interacting with recorded models to make practice more effective and efficient.

Let's hear it!: prerecorded models

Listening to a recording provides a roadmap—an aural "soundmap"—for the piece, setting the stage for future practice. Simply having the sound in your ear saves a lot of learning time. Recordings also provide motivation early in the learning process, when the sound coming from the student's instrument may be slow and incomplete.

Repertoire selection itself can be facilitated by using recordings. Rather than teachers assigning pieces, they can suggest several appropriate choices. Students can then listen to recordings and choose which piece they like best. This gives students ownership, and they will be more internally motivated to practice their chosen work.

Once a piece is selected, teachers may choose a specific recording to share with students or take advantage of the multiple interpretations available at their fingertips. To avoid students becoming too set in the interpretation of the recording, teachers may ask students to evaluate different recordings—try for at least three—with different stylistic interpretations. YouTube has historical, professionally produced, performances, as well as many performances by amateurs or students of similar ability levels to students' own. Comparing and contrasting these interpretations opens up multiple teaching opportunities. It's important for teachers to take the time in lessons to discuss interpretive possibilities, and teachers can guide students toward the more successful models.

Further, students can sometimes hear a problem easier in someone else's performance, and it is often easier for students to understand a musical point when they hear both a good and a subpar performance side by side. For instance, video examples of good and poor string vibrato may help students better understand the appropriate motions behind the technique.

Listening during lessons encourages students to listen at home. As we've mentioned earlier, students generally do at home what they've done in their lessons.[8]

YouTube and other online resources can help restore a curiosity in the music students are studying. Once students start searching, YouTube will suggest related videos, which opens students' eyes and ears to other possibilities. This may lead them to alternate interpretations or even new repertoire choices. Some students will really connect with the emotional content of the piece. Asking students to listen and create a storyline or image about the music can deepen this connection.

When using various sources, websites like Pinterest allow students and teachers to collect their favorite performances in one place. Additional information about the pieces being learned (e.g., history, photos, art, recordings, technical information) can also be pinned to a Pinterest board (see Figure 3.1).[9] These boards may include fun, extramusical information about the piece or related music as well as helpful educational material and recordings. This is a fun activity and focuses the students' attention on the music or composer they are studying.

Let me show you: teacher-recorded models

Today's recording technology allows teachers to expand the use of modeling beyond the studio walls. Demonstrating a technique, tone, or interpretation is a tried-and-true way of communicating musical ideas to students, and most teachers demonstrate short passages naturally during the course of a lesson. Recording these models is easy on either the teacher's or student's cell phone. This allows students to take the recorded model home with them and listen or watch the example multiple times. Teachers can even record an example following the lesson if an idea comes to mind later or if lesson time ran short. Initially it does take time for teachers to record models, but most recordings can be used over and over with many different students.

For teaching purposes, the quality of recording apps, even most voice recording apps, is acceptable. However, adding a microphone can quickly enhance audio quality. The book *Recording Tips for Music Education: A Practical Guide for Recording School Groups* by Ronald E. Kearns is a helpful reference for teachers interested in learning about advanced recording techniques.[10]

With many pieces, teachers can anticipate where students will need help and create audio or video recordings that model a particular problem or technique. Some teachers even create full lessons on a technique or a piece that are shared online.[11] Tutorials can be

Vivaldi Four Seasons
27 Pins

FIGURE 3.1 Author-created example of a Pinterest board for Vivaldi's *Four Seasons*, showing musical and extramusical information about the pieces.

short (two to ten minutes) and on any topic the teacher finds valuable. These lessons are particularly effective for techniques that teachers cover frequently and repetitively (e.g., instrument position, breathing). Teachers only have the time to model a technique once or twice during a lesson, but students can watch video tutorials at home as many times as needed. Teachers can decide whether to make the content public or available only to their students. Teachers may also record etudes and pieces taught by ear (e.g., fiddle music), as there may not be prerecorded models for the students to listen to.

To structure students' practice routines, teachers can record practice how-to videos (or audio-only recordings). For instance, a teacher might record a five- to ten-minute warm-up or an entire practice routine. Students can play along with this recording, which keeps them focused, and they are less likely to leave out important steps. We'll talk more about the benefits of playing along with recordings in the next section, but generally playing along with a recording is more enjoyable, especially for technical work like scales and chord progressions.[12]

To share self-recorded models, teachers can take advantage of social media by creating studio- or class-specific pages (for example a YouTube channel, Facebook page, or studio blog). Live streaming is even an option on some social media, for instance Facebook Live, but a simple email attachment works as well.

No longer do teachers have to be in the same room with the student to provide an aural model. Now, students can have a model they are able to listen to repeatedly, ensuring they fully grasp the technique or interpretation being practiced.

Flipping the lesson

A current educational trend is the "flipped classroom," where students watch video lessons at home and put their learning to practical use in the classroom.[13] Adding video tutorials for the students to watch at home adds to already interactive music classes and lessons.

Tutorials can also be used to extend lessons to include topics that are musically valuable, but are often left out because of time. For instance, historical and theoretical information about a piece of music is valuable, but teachers sometimes prioritize technical issues. Teachers can create a five-minute video on the composer and historical context of a piece, which can be watched by all students who will eventually play the piece.

Teachers may not even have to create videos themselves, as another teacher may have already made a quality tutorial publically available through a YouTube channel or blog.[14] There are even full courses available for purchase, such as eNovativePiano.[15] Teachers may embrace these tutorials especially if they are well done, fit with the teacher's philosophy, and discuss issues that the teacher knows are common problems that need repeated attention.

Flipped classrooms traditionally include video, but step-by-step guides are also valuable. These guides can include photos, audio, and video recordings to highlight each step. Teachers can post these tutorials on a studio blog or other website. Many teachers write blogs, so it's possible that information already exists on common technical issues.

Don't worry about these tutorials replacing one-to-one teaching. In a flipped classroom, it's important to have both video tutorials and teacher interaction. Most students need a teacher to help guide them.

Come play with me: playing with recordings

Playing along with recordings takes students a step beyond just listening to an aural model. As mentioned in chapter 1, it's important to develop a picture of the whole piece before breaking it down into sections for intensive practice. This is particularly difficult for ensemble players, where an individual part may not capture the whole flavor of the piece. Current technology makes this practice strategy much easier with smaller and more powerful speakers and wireless headsets that don't impede playing.

Students can make surprising leaps in their progress after only a couple of times of playing along with a recording.

Numerous apps such as Amazing Slow Downer exist that can adjust the tempo of recordings while maintaining desired pitch. With slowdowner apps, students can play with a recording even if their own playing isn't yet up to performance speed. As discussed in chapter 2, slowdowner apps can function like metronomes, practicing slow to fast, but within a musical context. The Amazing Slow Downer app even has a loop feature, which makes finding and saving difficult passages easy for a return visit (see Figure 3.2). Vocalists may also find this app particularly useful to transpose pitch without changing tempo.

Since slowdowner apps work with any mp3 file, teachers can record their own models and students can play along, at a slower tempo, with the teacher.

There are numerous ways to use the practice strategy of playing along with recordings. We'll discuss two: sight reading with a recording to find the passages that need practice, and playing with an accompaniment track.

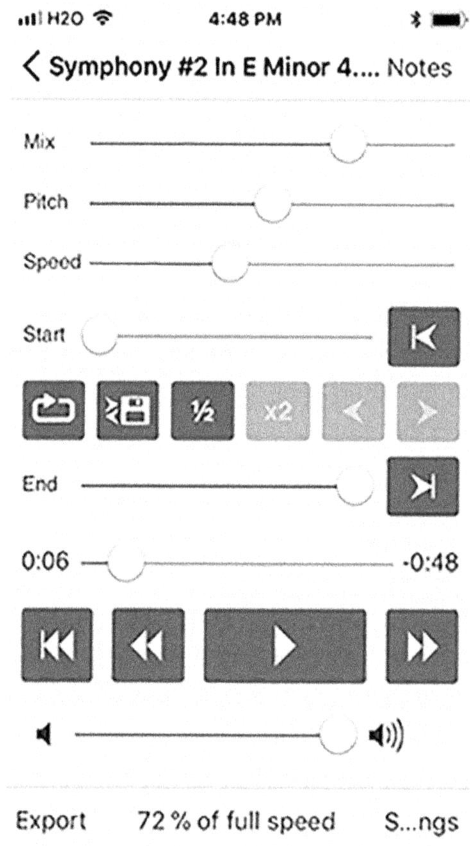

FIGURE 3.2 Screenshot of the Amazing Slow Downer app showing a forty-nine-second loop of Rachmaninov's *Symphony #2*, 4th movement, playing at 72 percent speed.

BOX 3.1 Visit the companion website

See the companion website 3.1 for a video demonstration of the loop feature on the Amazing Slow Downer.

BOX 3.2 Visit the companion website

See the companion website 3.2 and 3.3 for videos of a university student, Morgan T. McCullough, using the Amazing Slow Downer app to practice for her group piano class.

Sight reading by ear

Sight reading with a recording allows students to quickly form an aural overview of the piece and prioritize what needs practicing. After all, research shows that aural expectations are key to successful sight reading.[16] Playing with a recording is actually very similar to sight reading with a metronome. Students match their performance with an external sound source. However, the recording provides a realistic musical context (e.g., rubato, accompaniment) without the annoying "tick," which students can easily ignore.

When playing with a recording, students can easily hear when they "fall off"—where the music keeps going without them. These are the passages that will need more work. It's important to teach students a system for marking the places that need practicing (e.g., checkmarks, stars, brackets). Students might be surprised at how much music they can already sight read at tempo. No need to waste time practicing these passages!

In cases where the music is simply too difficult to be sight read at tempo, students can either follow the score or part while listening to the recording or use a slowdowner app to sight read at a slower tempo. Even at the slower tempo, students are continuing to develop an aural model of the piece and establishing practice and performance goals.

Sight reading with a recording helps push the student forward in the music. This is particularly helpful for students who hesitate and stop at their first mistake. Some students have difficulty pushing to the end, but the recording propels a student through a place they would normally stop.

Playing along with a recording as a practice strategy is useful throughout the various stages of practice as a way to check progress. For instance, after working intensively on a passage, playing with a recording allows the student to find places they still fall off. These are the places that need additional practice.

Music minus one

Playing with an accompaniment track, a recording that doesn't include the solo part, forces students to be independent and place their part into the full musical context. Ideally, students should play along with accompaniments early in the learning process. This allows students to make informed musical decisions about issues like breathing and phrasing, and not be distracted by the additional sound when a live accompaniment is added later. However, most students don't have constant access to an accompanist. Technology bridges the gap, allowing students to prepare for collaborative performance earlier in the process.

Most major method books and curricular sequences like the Associated Board of the Royal Schools of Music (ABRSM) provide accompaniment tracks in the form of mp3s or CDs. Specialized music apps like SmartMusic also exist that include accompaniments.[17] Designing accompaniment apps that follow the performer is the challenge. This technology is currently incorporated into programs like Piano Maestro and others that use MIDI, such as Home Concert Xtreme.[18] Piano Maestro visually tracks the musical notation as students play.[19] The program stops if the performer stops. We look forward to more widespread development on this key feature of accompaniment programs.

Made-to-order accompaniments can easily be created by the teacher or an accompanist using mobile devices. The benefit is that these can include personalized interpretations including rubato and tempo, but even if an interpretation changes, existing apps like the Amazing Slow Downer and Audacity allow tempos to be selectively adjusted.[20] Students can play along with these recordings in between sessions with their accompanist.

In this section, we've been talking about the magic of modeling and using the recording technology to expand the use of traditional teaching and practicing techniques. Continuing the idea of recording, we'll now explore the benefits of recording full lessons—and how to help students use these recordings to improve their playing.

BOX 3.3 Visit the companion website

▶ See the companion website 3.4 for a video tutorial on how to download an accompaniment from YouTube and edit the tempo using Audacity.

Instant replay: benefits of recording lessons

Recording lessons allows students to bring their teacher home with them. Students can replay any modeling that happened during the lesson and hear feedback and reminders given by the teacher. Essentially, recording a lesson makes sure that the students accurately remember what was discussed. Research shows that recorded models sent home with students helped them practice.[21]

Students can always do more with the help of the teacher than they can on their own.[22] Recording the lesson helps students hear their own highest potential, motivating them to work harder.

It's important that the recording process be easy and become a habit that's integral to the lesson. The simplest way to record is to use the student's phone or tablet, though some teachers may prefer a higher-quality recording system. The benefit of recording on the student's device is that it's instantly accessible.

To ensure that the students are listening to the recorded lesson, some teachers have students write a detailed summary to turn in. This truly reinforces what has been discussed and worked on during the lesson. Students have a deeper ownership when they verbalize or write about the material. These reflections can take many forms, even a short tweet or a Facebook posting. Joe Alessi describes his system using email in Box 3.4.

Teachers can also use recordings during a lesson to help students self-assess. Students can sometimes hear or see a problem in a recording that they don't notice while playing, because they are often focused on the technical demands of the piece. For instance, students may believe they are playing with big dynamic contrast, but recording a

BOX 3.4 From a performer and teacher

All my students are required to record all their lessons. A written synopsis, emailed to me, should be sent before the next lesson. You can tell who the good students are because they thoroughly state the points and concepts covered in the lesson. It does pay off, because everything's written down and documented and into the future. This saves lots of time in the lesson because I know that they will listen to the lesson recording. It takes time to write things in the students' parts, and they should do it themselves after listening. Otherwise, it will distract from playing. We want to play and get a lot done, and talk about music. If they record everything, they notate things down the next day when they practice. What's also important is the student will hear themselves playing and also hear when I demonstrate.

—Joe Alessi, principal trombonist, New York Philharmonic and Julliard faculty passage may reveal the reality to be quite different. Teachers can easily help students self-assess by playing back the lesson recording and asking students to reflect on their playing.

Students' own reflection is much more powerful than a teacher repeatedly giving feedback. This takes time in a lesson, but students verbalizing what they hear or see is the key to internalizing their musical goals. This strategy models for students how to self-assess during their own weekly practice. Additionally, listening to lesson recordings adds variety and extends the students' attention span.

Pianists may have access to other recording tools, such as a digitally reproducing acoustic piano (e.g., Disklavier) or an electronic keyboard with a recording feature.[23] Digitally reproducing acoustic pianos record and play back key and pedal movement as well as sound. This adds another dimension to recorded playback. Advancements in the technology easily allow for long-distance teaching and modeling. We'll talk more about distance teaching in chapter 5.

Recording lessons also keeps a running record of progress. Students can easily forget or lose track of the progress they have made from week to week. Comparing a current performance with a previous performance from last week or last month can be highly motivating.

Teachers may be hesitant to record lessons for a variety of reasons—possibly because of the extemporaneous element of lessons—but most concerns are outweighed by the students' ability to review lesson material at home. Students may need to be encouraged to take the time to listen to lesson recordings at home. In Box 3.5, Jane Magrath talks about the best time during the week to listen to lesson recordings.

Before leaving this section, let's turn the tables and talk about the benefits of *teachers* listening to recorded lessons. This helps teachers assess their own teaching skills and whether their approach is working with each student. One thing to watch for is the ratio of teacher talk to student play. Ideally, the ratio should be at least 40/

BOX 3.5 From a performer and teacher

I learned that it was important to listen to the recording at the right time during the week. It's my suggestion that students would listen to it two or three days after the lesson—not the very next day. The first day should be devoted to the student's interpretation of the lesson. By the third or fourth day, most students will need a refresher of the sound and tone the teacher was going for or subtle changes the teacher encouraged the student to make.

I think what would surprise students the most is that I could discern if they listened to the lesson during the week. Those students that did listen moved head over heels faster than other students.

—Jane Magrath, piano pedagogy professor, University of Oklahoma

60.[24] A simple stopwatch or time tracking app like Toggl can help teachers quickly assess if they are talking too much during lessons.[25] Teachers can also listen for whether explanations were clear and whether there are additional performance issues that weren't initially addressed.

Musical selfies: recording home practice

Selfies are all the rage, so why not have students take a musical selfie?

Musical selfies are "snapshots" of recorded practice. A musical selfie is a self-recording of daily practice or a performance. It's just like a photo selfie, except that music is dynamic—it happens over time. Students can take short musical selfies, recording a short passage or phrase, or longer musical selfies that might be entire hour-long practice sessions. Just like photos, students can easily create musical selfies on their mobile devices.[26]

Some recording programs like Collabra allow students to record all home practicing.[27] These are long musical selfies. This type of program tracks student practice time, but also what the student is actually doing during that time. Collabra records practice videos, and both students and the instructor can make comments directly on the video. The teacher can click on a student comment and go right to that portion of the video, allowing them to provide midweek feedback. Checking the practice videos of a few students each week, even short sections, provides a window into students' learning process.

We often share selfies on social media, and musical selfies are no different. Students can share musical selfies with the teacher or their peers on a studio- or class-specific Facebook or Instagram page. In chapter 5, we'll talk more about leveraging social media to help students learn their music better.

Musical selfies encourage students to become independent learners. The next three sections present various strategies to help students effectively use their musical selfies.

Slow perfect recording

A *slow perfect recording* (or "slow best recording") of a passage or piece is a specific type of musical selfie assigned by the teacher. The students choose any tempo they wish as long as they play the notes correctly without hesitations.

To be successful, students need to listen to their recording and decide if they have played the music perfectly. They can rerecord if necessary at a slower tempo. Inevitably, students end up practicing more to create a slow perfect musical selfie.

These slow recordings are perfect models of the piece without hesitations, and provide the teacher and the student a baseline performance.

Creating the slow perfect recording is only the first step; these recordings serve as aural models, made more powerful because they are created by the students themselves.

Though recorded slowly, slowdowner apps allow students to hear their recordings at a faster tempo—making them "speedupper" apps. At this point in the student's practice, there is a gap between how fast the student can actually play and the ultimate performance tempo. Increasing their slow tempo to hear themselves play at performance tempo through the app can be incredibly motivating, and make the performance tempo seem possible.

Once students have created their slow perfect recording, it's time to play along!

Using the slow perfect recording as the aural model, students can play along with themselves at increasingly faster tempos. This is a simple yet powerful variation on the common metronome practice strategy.

Practicing highlights: edited recordings

Asking students to find short musical selfies within a longer personal recording forces student to make thoughtful choices. Similar to sport highlights, students share only the best, worst, or quirkiest moments from the week's practice sessions. This is a fun way to encourage students to watch and listen carefully to their practice recordings. It also doesn't swamp the teacher with lengthy recordings to assess.

Another approach follows a scavenger hunt idea. Students look for specific elements in their practice recordings. The teacher can ask for anything that needs special attention. For instance:

- best staccato articulation
- best bow hold or posture
- best play through with most effective dynamics
- best performance of specific lesson item: scales, passage, repertoire
- passage that needs the most work
- passage that is most improved (before-and-after pair where initial problems were fixed)

Logistically, it makes sense to keep the editing simple by using programs such as Audacity or Quicktime, or the built-in editing features on many mobile devices. If the current technology is still too advanced for students, have them simply identify places in the recording by referencing timings.

The important part is that students watch and reflect on their practice.

BOX 3.6 Visit the companion website

▶ See the companion website 3.6 for a tutorial on how to create edited highlights using Quicktime.

Blogging, vlogging, and podcasting: writing or speaking about practice

Asking students to reflect on their musical selfies is the most direct way of finding out what the student has learned. By writing or talking about their practice, students organize their ideas and think more deeply about what they are hearing. Teachers can use today's blogging, vlogging,[28] and podcasting technology to make writing or speaking about practice much more fun and interesting.

Before we continue, there are a couple of general points we should make about effective journaling. Students may try to write their reflections based on memory rather than listening to their recordings. Directing students toward a specific issue or problem like phrasing to write about can avoid this tendency. The focus may change from week to week, depending on the music.

Description and reflection are both important when journaling. Students can start with a description—what happened—during their practice. For instance, a student may observe tempo fluctuations during practice. Sometimes observing a problem is all that is needed to fix it. Reflection is a deeper level of self-analysis. Was the tempo appropriate? What strategies can be used to overcome hesitations?

Some students will have a tendency to dwell on mistakes—more so even than the teacher.[29] Asking the students to start their discussion with what went well helps counteract this tendency and is a positive way of approaching the learning process.

Blogging

Writing about practice can take many forms, including a personal blog, an email to the teacher, or a social media post (e.g., on a studio- or class-specific Twitter or Facebook page). Online, there are many examples of teachers blogging about pedagogy, but few blogs created by students or performing musicians. Blogs can be a powerful way for students to explore their musical journey.

Blogs need not be lengthy. Students can write one or two sentences about their practice session or even create lists ("Top Ten Things that Went Well in Practice"), getting to the point quickly. On the flip side, teachers can ask for longer blog postings. The word count is arbitrary, but usually asking for around five hundred words encourages students to relisten to their recording to find something more to say.

Some apps allow students to write directly into their recorded practice videos, time-stamping the comments. Teachers can see exactly what the student was reacting to and they can add their own comments into the video. We introduced Collabra earlier in the chapter, but other apps like iCoach and VideoNot.es have a similar video comment feature.[30] Figure 3.3 shows a student practicing the double bass and comments made by both the student and the teacher. The video focuses only on the students' hands.

Students can create musical selfies, adding sound or video files to their blog posting to demonstrate their points.

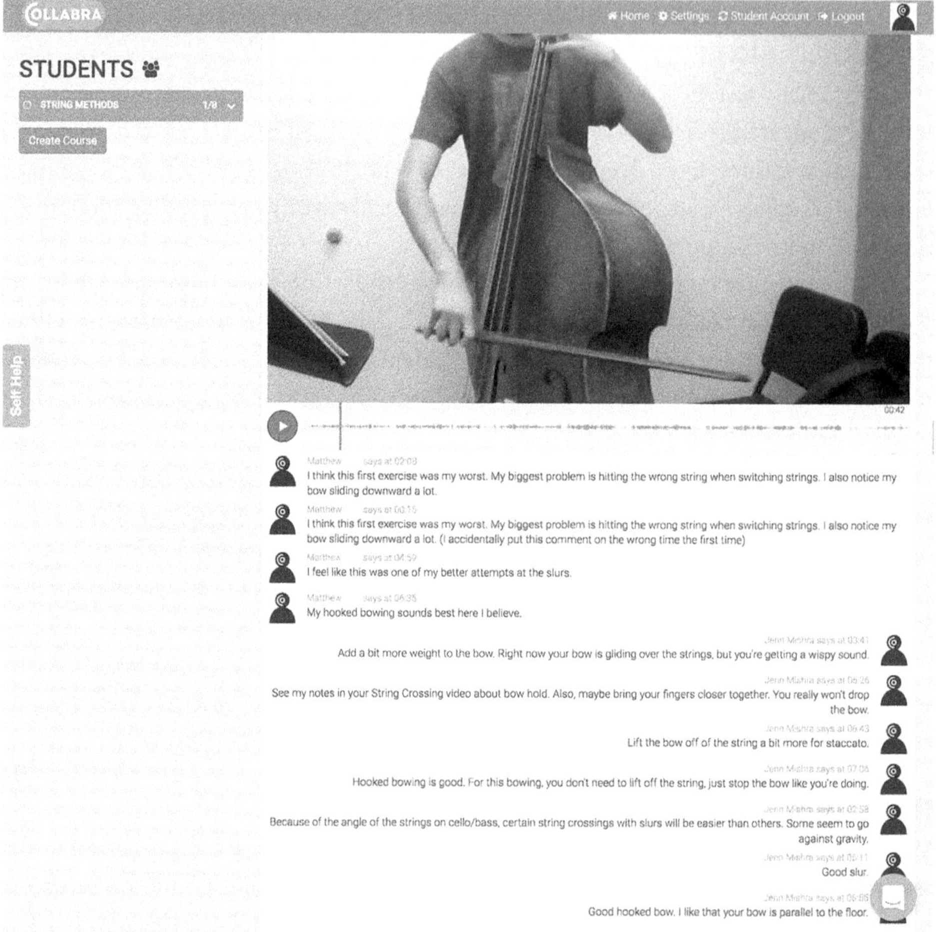

FIGURE 3.3 Screenshot of Collabra website showing comments between student and teacher about a submitted practice video. Comments are time-stamped and coordinated with the video.

> **BOX 3.7 Visit the companion website**
>
> Visit the companion website 3.7 for a review of some video editing programs useful in musical practice.

Vlogging and podcasting

Musical selfies can easily expand into vlogging and podcasting where students talk, rather than write, about their practicing. For some students, this is a more natural approach.

The recording process need not be difficult. YouTube, Facebook, and Instagram make it easy to record directly into a computer or phone camera, and any audio or video file can be shared as a podcast. This can be expanded by asking students to write a short caption or even a mini-blog post to describe their recording.

Some students benefit from talking *during* practice in a stream-of-consciousness way—saying whatever comes to mind without censorship. This can include what the performer *wants* to be thinking about, self-reminders, and points of emphasis or visualizations. Sometimes students are surprised by what they notice. Gabriela Imreh, researcher and pianist, used this procedure to study her own practicing of the third movement of Bach's *Italian Concerto*, BWV 971.[31]

Alternatively, if two recording devices are available (e.g., computer, along with tablet or phone), students can play back their practice recordings on one device while recording their observations on the other. These procedures have the advantage of knowing what students are noticing in real time.

Musical selfies can be recordings of either practice sessions or a performance. In the next section, we'll talk about using recordings to prepare for performance and the new trend of expanding performance into the online venue.

iPerform: dress rehearsals, auditions and virtual recitals

Technology is changing our approach to live performances, including the way we prepare and share performances. Live performances are core to the musical experience and we don't see these being replaced with technology. However, used well, technology, like live streaming, can expand and enhance live performances in a number of ways.

Recording to perform: the digital dress rehearsal

Creating musical selfies throughout the learning process naturally leads to using self-recording as a tool in preparation for performance. Specifically, recordings can highlight whether the interpretation is effective and if there are any weak spots in the performance. Video recordings can additionally illuminate physical or technical ticks like facial expressions and body language, or highlight if students are moving in a distracting way. Ideally, these recordings are made in the full performance context: in program order, in performance attire, in the venue, and so on.

A variation on this idea is the "cold start recording." This means walking into a room and playing a piece, at tempo, without any warm-ups. There are no do-overs in performance—the first time counts! Different from the slow perfect recording described earlier, making a one-shot recording at tempo is an easy way to mimic a performance situation. Recording without a warm-up simulates the time and location gap between warm-ups and performance. Additionally, fingers and embouchure feel different because of the tension associated with performance—more like playing without any warm-up time.

For many people, recording a performance simulates the performance anxiety of a concert setting.[32] This may be one reason why students are hesitant to record themselves without a teacher's suggestion. Recording a performance every day helps some musicians overcome this anxiety. Some musicians (even professionals) find it difficult to listen to their performances and assess their own playing. If students get in the habit of recording and listening to themselves, they won't develop this reluctance.

Recording practice can help prepare for performance, but this strategy can also be used for formal evaluation purposes.

High-tech tests: assessments and auditions

Many teachers are using recorded performances (or assigned excerpts) as part of their overall assessment strategy. These are particularly valuable for ensemble directors and group classes, where time does not allow for frequent individual evaluations. Teachers have several choices when assigning recorded playing tests.

Some teachers block time in class for students to record their tests in an office or practice room; others allow students to record at home. Home recording allows for more student independence, but requires that all students also be self-motivated and have basic recording technology. Teachers must also decide whether students can rerecord or not. The benefit of allowing students to rerecord is that it encourages them to listen and assess each attempt—and they usually end up practicing more.

There are many options for how recorded playing tests can be submitted to teachers. One major benefit of SmartMusic is the ease of submission and assessment. Other teachers use common online sharing strategies ranging from a simple email attachment (though files can be large), to Dropbox or YouTube videos. YouTube videos can be uploaded as "unlisted" videos (i.e., unsearchable) for privacy. Increasingly less common is the submission of CDs and DVDs, as the technology is currently moving away from these formats. A low-tech variation is for students to call a specially created Google Voice phone number and record their playing tests directly into the phone.[33] It's a matter of finding a format that is comfortable and easy to use.

Regardless of how students submit their recordings, teachers need to develop a system of organization. This can be as simple as creating a free dedicated email account (concertband1playingtests@mail.com) or Dropbox folder.

A discussion of grading the playing tests is beyond the scope of this text, but there are a number of online rubric creation websites that may be helpful for teachers.[34]

Recorded auditions, like playing tests, are becoming more and more common as the technology has advanced, especially in terms of quality and ease of use. It has become standard practice that preliminary rounds of auditions for many orchestras, schools, and competitions are submitted via video. The National Association of Teachers of Singing (NATS), for instance, calls their preliminary round of auditions their "YouTube Round."[35] Final rounds are still generally live auditions. It is possible that as recording quality continues to improve, more auditions will be accepted via video.

Enhancing live performance

Technology has the ability to enhance live concerts through multimedia, hybrid, and live-streamed performances.

Concerts expanded

Multimedia concerts and recitals include arts and media, often presented through technology, that enhance a live performance. These types of concerts foster a deeper understanding of the music for performers and add interest for the audience. In the next couple of paragraphs, we'll present a few ideas that use technology to get the creative ideas flowing—multimedia concerts can be infinitely imaginative!

Projecting photos, text, or artwork on a screen behind or next to the performers is a creative and fun way of adding visuals to the music.[36] The images can be candid or posed photos of the performers or pictures chosen by the students to represent their piece. Short quotes or program-note style text can also be added or even presented in a more graphic way, for instance as a Wordle (see chapter 2). Younger students especially benefit from drawing pictures that represent the patterns in the music or a story that helps develop their interpretation. Students can share photos of the drawing process and the finished artwork with the audience (see Figure 3.4).[37]

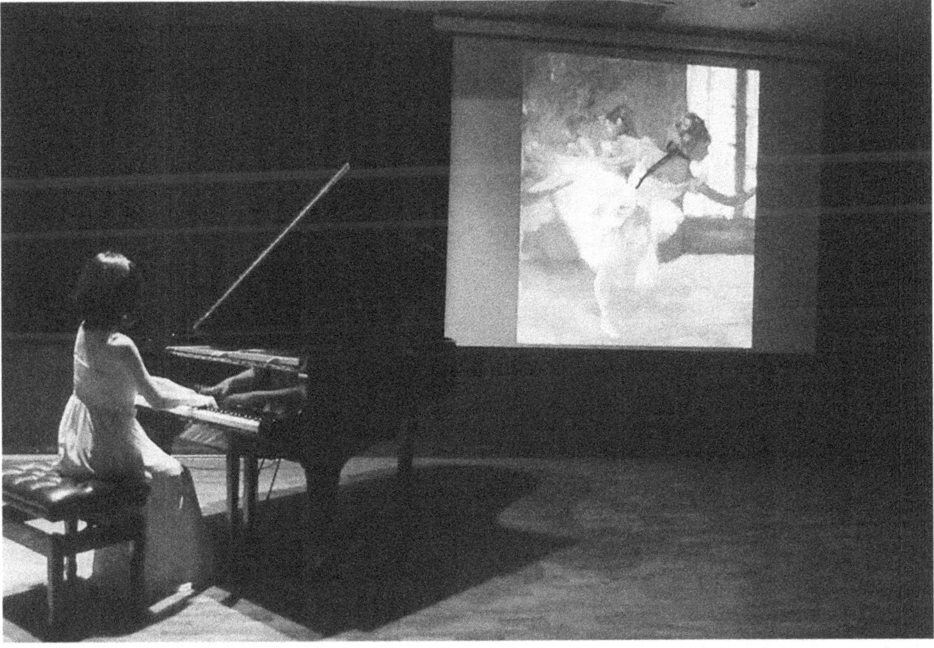

FIGURE 3.4 Student performs a piece by Debussy while an Impressionistic painting by Degas is projected on the screen. Photo used by permission of photographer Bert Boden.

Any type of slideshow program, such as PowerPoint or Keynote, will help the teacher organize photos for presentation, but most current photo apps also allow the easy creation of slideshows.

Another alternative is projecting an image onto a green screen set up behind the performer.[38] Green screen technology allows a solid green background to be replaced by another projected background image without obscuring the performer. This technology is often used in weather reporting and movie special effects. The image projected can be anything from a photo representing the mood or style of the piece, a performance venue like a grand concert hall, or a fanciful setting (even outer space!). Silent videos are also an option.

Adding video is easier than ever with simple video editing programs (e.g., Quicktime, iMovie). Students can record themselves talking about the pieces they are performing, or being interviewed by the teacher or a peer. For instance, students can talk about what they like about the piece, challenges they overcame during practice, and describe for the audience what to listen for in their piece. This is a personalized extension of traditional program notes.

There are many benefits to using prerecorded videos during performance. Many students will feel more comfortable video recording their thoughts ahead of time rather than speaking live during the concert. Further, teachers can better control content and time. These types of videos work well as transitions in between pieces or performers.

Earlier in this chapter, we explored vlogging and podcasting as ways of reflecting on the music. These already created videos or sound bites can provide interesting content in a concert setting.

Hybrid and virtual performances

Hybrid recitals include a video-recorded performance alongside live performances. These differ from multimedia concerts, as at least some of the live performances are replaced with video-recorded performances.

There are a couple of instances where hybrid recitals are useful. Hybrid recitals can include performances by students who, for whatever reason, can't attend the live performance (e.g., due to illness or travel). Hybrid recitals can also include prerecorded performances that show progress. For instance, videos taken at sight reading or during the early stages of learning show how far the student has progressed. Teachers implementing the musical selfie idea presented above will have plenty of footage to choose from. Teachers might also purposefully choose videos that lessen the formality of the traditional recital—for instance, showing fun student interaction.

Live performance can also be supplemented with live video projecting the performer on a larger screen. This gives the audience a more detailed view of the performer's face or hands.

In a virtual recital, performances are all recorded ahead of time and presented online. These can provide a different experience for the students. Virtual recitals can

BOX 3.8 From a teacher

Each of my students records one piece in my studio. We usually record a couple weeks during our regular lesson time. It's very informal and gives the kids something to work toward early in the year. I post to my YouTube channel and create a playlist. I do a program with a fun short bio for each student.

I ask each student to listen to at least ten different performances and circle which performances they heard. I also ask them to mark their favorites and bring their program to their next lesson. I save the programs and often check what the favorites were when I'm planning programs for the next year.

I make the playlist public for about three weeks so the kids can share their performances with grandparents and anyone else.

I went to this format because everyone can participate. I have more formal recitals later in the year. This has been a fun goal to work toward early in the year. Students are so busy and have so many conflicts I didn't want to schedule another formal recital. I wanted a different experience.

—Roberta Quist, independent piano teacher

accomplish similar goals as a live performance. Students have a goal to work toward, and recording the performance can often produce as much anxiety as a live recital.

As schedules become more complicated and venues more difficult to book, some teachers have begun considering at least one virtual recital a year (for instance a virtual recital in December and a live recital in May). Box 3.8 is a quote from piano teacher Roberta Quist, who has successfully used virtual recitals. She recorded student performances during lesson time, although other teachers may feel comfortable with home recordings.

As mentioned in Box 3.8, virtual recitals are also a natural way of archiving a performance, which can be shared with relatives and friends who would not be able to attend a live performance.

Live streaming

Increasingly more common is the option to live-stream performances. This allows performances to be shared, in real time, to a wider audience. For instance, this allows access for family members who are unable to travel to the performance. This type of recording retains all of the anticipation of a live performance, with the added bonus that it can be shared and archived for later viewing.

Many professional venues, including concert halls and universities, are making concerts available through live streaming, expanding access exponentially beyond the walls of the concert hall.[39]

Live streaming provides a new way of interacting with the performers. Those watching the live stream can often comment or send emojis on what they are seeing and hearing. This feature has benefits of allowing the audience to interact with each other and (later) the performers. Comments also provide insight for performers to understand their audiences' reactions. However, teachers might be cautious of allowing comments, at least unedited comments, on their feed since not all may be positive.

Conclusion

Students who constantly listen to themselves will develop confidence in their sound and who they are as musicians. Today's technology allows students to easily record their practice sessions, whether recording just a few minutes or hours of practicing. These musical selfies allow students to truly evaluate how they sound and to monitor their progress over time. Technique is important and foundational, but at the end of the day, performance depends on our ears—hearing what we want to produce or play. Recordings allow us to step back from the technique of producing the sound and truly evaluate the musical effect on its own.

Students today have been raised as the YouTube generation, and teachers can use these musical models to open up discussion. Technology also allows teachers to easily record and share their own models with students. Further, recording lessons allows students to bring their teacher home with them, ensuring that daily practice is effective.

Virtual auditions and performance take the idea of self-recording to the next level. Technology can even expand what we think of as a traditional recital. As we mentioned earlier, live performances are core to the musical experience and we don't see these being replaced with technology, but we live in a time when the traditional concert hall has the potential to be more accessible, innovative, and exciting.

Notes

1. Research by Nancy Barry and Victoria McArthur shows that in 1994, few teachers required students to audio or video record their practicing or even listen to models. However, much has changed in the world of technology in the intervening years. Their findings are published in the article "Teaching Practice Strategies in the Music Studio."
2. Admittedly, there have been historical limitations of recording technology. Formats frequently changed, technology was clumsy, time consuming, and expensive. Early on, recordings were a novelty and the quality and access to this technology was limited. Many music teachers embraced portable devices (e.g., cassette recorders, DVD players) as they became more accessible and affordable, but they still required a dedicated purchase.
3. The Arlen Fast quote comes from research by Jennifer Mishra and Barbara Fast in "Practising in the New World."
4. Musician Nancy Barry and music psychologist Susan Hallam wrote a comprehensive and easy to understand overview of musical practice from a research perspective in the chapter "Practice" in Richard Parncutt and Gary McPherson's book *The Science and Psychology of Music Performance*.

5. Shinichi Suzuki's philosophies are documented in his book *Nurtured By Love.*
6. YouTube is known as a video hosting service, but also includes audio-only files, including Naxos recordings.
7. One option for downloading mp3 files from YouTube is www.vidtomp3.com, though there are many other programs, websites, and browser plug-ins designed for this purpose.
8. See the Barry and Hallam chapter "Practice" in Richard Parncutt and Gary McPherson's book *The Science and Psychology of Music Performance* as well as Nancy Barry's 2007 research "A Qualitative Study of Applied Music Lessons and Subsequent Student Practice Sessions."
9. The Pinterest board for Vivaldi's Four Seasons may be found at www.pinterest.com/jenniferm7288/vivaldi-four-seasons.
10. See Ronald E. Kearns, *Recording Tips for Music Education.*
11. There are many good examples of recorded models online. For examples, see Todd Ehle's YouTube channel at www.youtube.com/user/professorV/about, and for tutorials using Instagram video go to www.instagram.com/vibrantviolincoaching.
12. An example of a professionally recorded warm-up routine with New York Philharmonic trombonist Joe Alessi may be found at www.youtube.com/watch?v=6UDy1viqTJA, and a beginning string example may be found at www.youtube.com/watch?v=jJ9CjiuUBOQ.
13. Bill Tucker introduces the topic of flipped classrooms in his article "The Flipped Classroom."
14. For instance, Professor Todd Ehle has made more than thirty violin tutorials publically available on his YouTube channel, covering everything from simple hand position to vibrato; see www.youtube.com/user/professorV/about. New York Philharmonic trombonist Joe Alessi has a series of videos at www.alessimusicstudios.com.
15. The eNovativePiano website is https://enovativepiano.com/about.
16. Jennifer Mishra presented research supporting the importance of aural expectations in sight reading in her article "Improving Sightreading Accuracy."
17. SmartMusic is discussed in more detail in chapter 2.
18. More information about the Home Concert Xtreme app may be found at https://itunes.apple.com/us/app/home-concert-xtreme/id443017184?mt=8.
19. More information about Piano Maestro and other apps by JoyTunes may be found at www.joytunes.com/apps.
20. Audacity is a free cross-platform recording and editing program. It may be downloaded at www.audacityteam.org/home.
21. There are a number of studies that support the use of aural models in practice. One such was published by Michael P. Hewitt "The Effects of Modeling, Self-Evaluation, and Self-Listening on Junior High Instrumentals' Music Performance and Practice Attitude."
22. This idea comes out of Vygotsky's "zone of proximal development," which states students can do more with the help of a teacher or a more experienced peer than they can do on their own. An overview of this idea may be found in Seth Chaiklin's chapter "The Zone of Proximal Development in Vygotsky's Analysis of Learning and Instruction," published in Alex Kozulin's book *Vygotsky's Educational Theory in Cultural Context.*
23. For more information about disklaviers, go to https://usa.yamaha.com/products/musical_instruments/pianos/disklavier/index.html.
24. Joseph Manfredo provides an overview of research on pacing rehearsals in his article "Effective Time Management in Ensemble Rehearsals."
25. Toggl is one of many time management apps. More information may be found at https://toggl.com.
26. Searching for hashtags such as #practicemusic, #musicpractice, or #musicalpractice will provide examples posted by musicians of all levels.
27. Collabra is a subscription-based service that hosts hours of practice recordings. More information may be found at https://wordpress.collabramusic.com.
28. A vlog is a video blog. A vlogger creates a video and shares it online, for instance on a YouTube channel.
29. Focusing on negative elements of practice is called "negativity bias." A good introduction to negativity bias may be found in the article by Roy Baumeister and colleagues, "Bad is Stronger than Good."

30. The iCoach app is designed for sports, and allows comments to be written directly onto a video. More information may be found at http://icoachapp.org. VideoNot.es annotates directly into a video using YouTube and Google Drive.
31. There are many published studies based on Gabriela Imreh's practicing, but the article "Pulling Teeth and Torture," published with Roger Chaffin, is focused on the comments that she made during practice.
32. For more information about performance anxiety, see Dianna Kenny's book *The Psychology of Music Performance Anxiety*.
33. We thank band director Matt McKeever for the useful idea of using Google Voice for playing tests.
34. For an introduction to writing music rubrics see Brian C. Wesolowski's article "Understanding and Developing Rubrics for Music Performance Assessment."
35. For details about YouTube Rounds see the NATS webpage at www.nats.org/national_student_auditions.html.
36. Adding artwork or text to a performance is becoming more common with professional ensembles. Performing film scores in a live concert with the movie playing in the background has also become an accepted and popular part of a concert series.
37. To see the original photo and to find out more about this particular concert, go to Bert Boden's blog at http://gbboden.com/blog/concerts/the-151st-debussys-anniversary.
38. For examples and tutorials created by teachers using green screens, go to Jennifer Stadler's YouTube channel www.youtube.com/channel/UCP-3_ffjfF982lEtS1W4RkQ or Leila Voss's website https://88pianokeys.me/studio-management/use-a-green-screen-for-virtual-performances.
39. A number of ensembles, such as the New York Philharmonic, live-stream concerts as well as behind the scenes videos on their Facebook page; see www.facebook.com/nyphilharmonic. The Proms, a large concert festival at the Royal Albert Hall in London, has concerts available online through BBC Radio 3 at www.bbc.co.uk/radio3.

4

Taking the Next Step

Using Notation Software in the Practice Room

Introduction

This chapter is about practicing the really difficult sections in music—the places that students flag, bracket, circle, highlight, and blanket with fingerings. These are the places that students come back to again and again during their practice; places that are confusing, awkward to play, hard to read, too fast, or just don't seem to make musical sense. In other words, practicing the passages that drive musicians mad!

Frustration sets in. No matter how many times students builds up the passage with a metronome or listens to the recording, they can't seem to play what's on the page. Students have seemingly tried everything; teachers have advocated every practice strategy they know. This is the point where teachers and students need to explore a new practicing strategy: a new tool for their toolbox.

In this chapter we will explore notation software as a possible next step, when other practice strategies have failed. This technology allows musicians to see and hear difficult passages in a totally different way. Composers, by and large, have embraced notation software, and teachers and students can too.

Practice parts

Before getting started, let's introduce the concept of a *practice part*. A practice part is a working document based on the original printed music. Making a practice part starts with entering music into a notation program like Finale, but simple, web-based programs such as Noteflight or MuseScore work just as well.[1] Practice parts are usually only excerpts

> **BOX 4.1 Visit the companion website**
>
> Many of the examples in this chapter were created using Noteflight at www.noteflight.com Visit the companion website 4.1 for reviews of notation software programs.

of the most difficult sections—a bar or two or a phrase or two—but the entire piece can be entered if desired.

Once the musical excerpt has been entered into the software, the student can easily change the visual look of the notation for better understanding. Let's be clear—we are advocating changing how the music *looks* on the page, not changing the actual *sound* of the composition. The concept of a practice part isn't really new. We write reminders into musical notation all the time: fingerings, metric hashes, bowings, accidentals—all general reminders. Practice parts just take this idea to the next level, making the score fully dynamic.[2]

Practice parts are changeable, but most importantly, practice parts are personal. A practice part for one student may be very close to the original score, while another student may want to change the look of the notation substantially.

But don't worry! Practice parts are only temporary. Students will normally only use practice parts in the practice room, during the learning process when they are working with a particularly difficult section. Once the passage is mastered, students can return to the original score. However, there are instances when it might be appropriate for a student to continue to use practice parts in performance—the audience will never know! Remember, the sound of the music is not changed.

Figure 4.1 is an example of a practice part created from an original engraved score of Marilyn Shrude's *Litanies*, measure 66 (first half). We'll discuss this example in more detail later in the chapter, but for now notice all of the possible changes that might be made to the notation when it is entered into a software program—and how much easier the re-notation is to read. To emphasize, even though these two examples look very different on the page, the actual music sounds the same.

The second example is much easier to read, but remember, there is a reason why the composer chose to write this passage in a nonmetric way, and it's important not to lose that characteristic in the final performance. The practice part simply allows for faster, easier learning.

In sections that follow, we will explore how practice parts can be used to help students understand the music on a deeper level, changing the score to fit personal tastes in how the notation looks. By sharing examples from our personal practice journeys, we hope to show the value of creating practice parts and inspire personal creativity in the practice room.

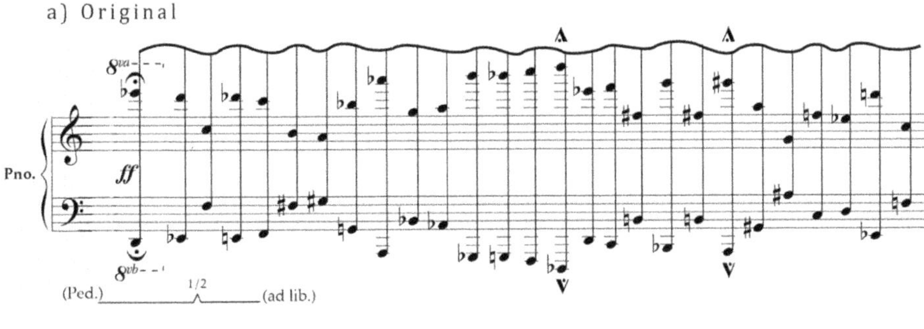

FIGURE 4.1 An excerpt (measure 66, first half) from the piano part of Marilyn Shrude's *Litanies*, originally scored for piano, flute, and oboe (example A). A practice part (example B) was created from the original engraving. Example used by permission of composer.

> **BOX 4.2 Visit the companion website**
>
> Go to the companion website 4.2 to hear this excerpt of *Litanies* by Marilyn Shrude.

The value of entering music into a notation program

Making a practice part starts with copying the musical excerpt into notation software. The more advanced programs have a scan feature that allows printed music to be uploaded directly into the program. This is a nice feature for quick entry, but it bypasses a valuable aspect in creating a practice part, as Arlen Fast describes in Box 4.3. The act of copying focuses students' attention on the details and the patterns in the music, making copying

BOX 4.3 From a performer

In the process of putting music into the computer, you begin to see certain patterns. I don't have to even hear it played back to know that I'm working with a pattern, because I'm watching for where things repeat. I may have to change one or two things along the way, but it's quick to copy and paste and then you begin to the see the patterns. And it's not a shock to read the double sharps when they come, because they lie in the patterns. Then when I listen to it, it confirms what I already learned from having put it in.

When I sit down to practice it, I don't have to dig out all the notes because they fall into patterns. Okay, so I get the idea it's like Strauss, but it's so chromatic it would be tedious to learn it by just looking at the notes. But if I hear it played back for me, I'm like "oh, I can do that."

—Arlen Fast, bassoonist, New York Philharmonic[3]

itself an important practice strategy. A thousand little details in the notation need to be observed and transferred into the software and a thousand little questions need to be answered: Is the note articulated with a dot? A dash? An accent? Where does the phrasing or crescendo mark begin and end? Is the pitch a natural or a sharp?

The performer needs to be aware of these details to accurately execute the music. Even the best musician sometimes overlooks an important articulation or dynamic marking during practice, and we all know that relearning the music can be much more difficult than learning it correctly in the first place. The amount of detail that needs to be included in a practice part really depends on the reason for the re-notation. Teachers can guide students in the appropriate amount of detail necessary. It may not be important to enter every dynamic change or articulation.

This process of copying isn't quick, but there is one important shortcut. Patterns come to light as the eye looks for quicker ways to enter the notation. When a repetition is found, encourage the use of the copy–paste features in the notation program. Copy–paste. Copy–paste–transpose. Each time a pattern is found, the student knows a little bit more about how the music is constructed (e.g., sequences, chord structure). Our brains like patterns. Patterns make everything simpler.

Entering the notation into the computer allows students to find patterns in the music, and this translates into finding technical patterns on the instrument—shortening the amount of time students need to physically practice. This process can open up musical and technical discussions between teacher and student. Can the same fingering be used when the pattern repeats? The same bowing? How can the repetitions be musically connected in the phrase?

BOX 4.4 From a musicologist

Beethoven copied Mozart's *String Quartet in G major* KV 387 . . . he did not copy the work in order to possess it (if this had been the case he could have bought the printed edition, which would have been simpler and quicker), but rather to study the compositional technique. . . . In order to have an overview of the structure and to understand the construction of the movement, for better or worse, Beethoven had to swallow the bitter pill and first of all produce a handwritten score. As additional markings such as dynamics and phrasing are not relevant for studying compositional technique, Beethoven did not bother copying them. . . . Beethoven copied many of the Salzburg composer's works to study their compositional style and structure, and in so doing to learn from Mozart.

—Julia Ronge, musicologist[4]

The idea of copying parts in order to learn the music more deeply isn't a new learning strategy, but it is one that has almost been forgotten. Composers like Bach and Vivaldi would have learned how to compose largely through copying parts of earlier masters. Musicologist Julia Ronge describes the process in Box 4.4.

Don't underestimate the educational value of copying music into a notation program. Sometimes attending to the minute details written in the score is all students need to take the music to the next level.

Now that the practice part is made, let's put it to work!

Aural model

The previous chapter focused on the importance of an aural model for students: "The ear guides the fingers. If you can hear it, you can play it." We emphasized obtaining a recording to hear the music and using apps such as the Amazing Slow Downer as a metronome substitute to slow down the recording.[5] Practice parts can be used in a similar way.

Notation programs generally allow for tempo manipulation and have the ability to play back the notated music. The sampled sound isn't always ideal, but current notation programs generally have acceptable timbres for the practice room.

Recordings work well for hearing solo works, but when playing ensemble music, it's not always easy for students to hear one part, especially in the middle of the texture. Notation programs allow one line of music to be isolated from the rest of the ensemble or any complex multivoice texture. Using a notation program to create an aural model is also particularly useful when practicing pieces that are newly composed or have not been recorded. Etudes or other technical exercises, for instance, are rarely recorded and yet a performer may benefit from hearing them.

Every feature of the music can be entered into the notation software and heard, but maybe there is just an awkward interval or a tempo transition that needs to be heard several times. A practice part doesn't need to include every feature of the original notation; it just needs to include the features that are needed to help students perform the piece better.

Figure 4.2 is an example of a complex transition with both a meter and tempo change. Entering a few notes into a notation program allows the music to be played back. Just hearing the transition a couple of times sets up an aural expectation.

Once we can hear it, we can play it.

Editors of published music sometimes add entrance cues to ensemble music. These cues help performers develop an expectation about how to fit their part into the texture of the whole ensemble. Notation software allows every musician to be an editor—adding as many cues as needed, not just the cues the editor thought were needed. Not only does the computer allow the musician to see the cue, but also to hear the cue in relation to his or her own part. Published cues are usually only provided during rests, but a notation program allows musicians to enter two or more parts to hear how they relate.

The computer has now become a tutor.

Taking this idea a step further, the musician can now play along with any other part or combination of parts of the ensemble. Once the student has gained confidence with playing along, the notation program allows parts to be silenced. Students can test themselves, with the computer providing the ensemble and the performer playing his or her part at the appropriate time.

Figure 4.3 was created to help fit the viola line into the quick opening of the 4th movement of Rachmaninov's *Symphony No. 2*, Op. 27.

Entrance cues are just one element that a musician might add from the score into a practice part. Maybe a student just needs to hear how a note is tuned as part of a chord.

FIGURE 4.2 Excerpt of measures 17–18 of the bassoon part of Ades's *In Seven Days*, 5th movement, showing a complex transition with both meter and time change. Example created in music notation program.

BOX 4.5 Visit the companion website

Go to the companion website 4.3 to hear the complex transition example.

FIGURE 4.3 Excerpt of measures 1–6 of Rachmaninov's *Symphony No. 2*, Op. 27, 4th movement, showing the viola part (bottom stave) and important orchestral cues (top stave). Example created in music notation program.

> **BOX 4.6 Visit the companion website**
>
> ▶ Go to the companion website 4.4 to hear a recorded performance of the Rachmaninov excerpt and the midi version of the viola part with cues.

Enter the chord into the software, listen, then remove one part from the chord and have the student play along, tuning with the computer. Off-beat patterns, especially if they are extended and at a fast tempo, can be tricky to practice. Downbeats can be entered into the software to provide stability—this basically creates a more realistic pitched metronome. Which leads us to click tracks.

Click tracks

Metronomes have improved greatly with the app explosion of the 21st century, but they still have limitations. Even practicing basic accelerandos and ritardandos, for instance, is impossible with most metronomes, but is simple to add in a notation program. Click tracks are simply metronomes created in notation programs, specific to a section of music where the meter or rhythm is too complex for a metronome.

Click tracks created in notation programs are more flexible than metronomes, allowing musicians to specify any tempo changes or meters. Let's return to the Ades example, a piece that includes a difficult musical transition (see Figure 4.4). As mentioned earlier, hearing the transition played by the computer is the first step to correctly

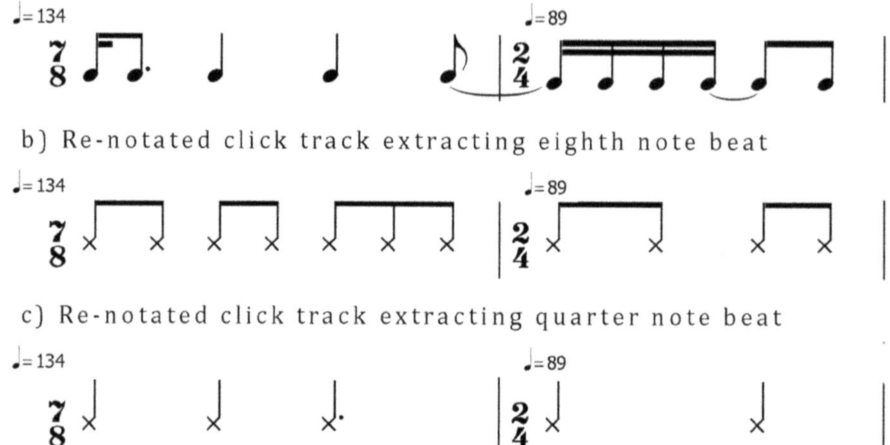

FIGURE 4.4 Click tracks created in a music notation program based on the rhythm of measures 17–18 of the bassoon part of Ades's *In Seven Days*, 5th movement (example A), extracting eighth note pulse (example B) and quarter note pulse (example C).

> **BOX 4.7 Visit the companion website**
>
> ▶ See the companion website 4.5 for a tutorial on how to create click tracks in a notation program.

performing the tempo and meter change. Stripping away the complex rhythms leaves just the beat—either eighth note beat or quarter note beat—using any preferred percussion timbre.

The computer becomes a specialized metronome—or click track—for practicing the change in tempo and meter between these two bars. This passage would be impossible to practice with most metronomes. Further, it is easy to loop this click track for repetitive practice. Simply, copy and paste the click track as many times as desired, and the computer will replay these two measures for practice.

Now that the click track has been created, it can be manipulated in various ways by students for practice. For instance, tempo can be adjusted within the loops (see Figure 4.5). Tempos can be as slow as desired as long as the relationship between the tempos stays the same. To practice this exercise at 50 percent speed, metronome markings would be changed to 67 and 45 respectively. Teachers may need to help students with this conversion, but once the click track is created students can practice a passage repeatedly, increasing tempo after every couple of repetitions without having to stop and reset a metronome.

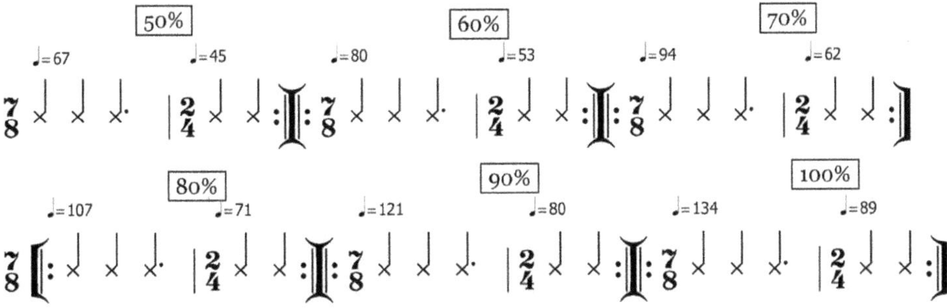

FIGURE 4.5 Click tracks created in a music notation program based on the rhythm of measures 17–18 of the bassoon part of Ades's *In Seven Days*, 5th movement, repeated at increasing faster tempos.

The Ades is a difficult example because of the tempo and meter change, but the same concept of programming in an increasingly faster tempo can be applied to simpler passages. This allows for a continuous stream of increasingly faster repetitions without the mental and physical pauses required when using a metronome.

Some students might benefit from additional manipulations to this click track. For instance, in the Ades example (Figure 4.2), the tempo changes from 134 to 89, but some students may find it helpful to play the meter change in isolation without the tempo change (playing both bars at 134) a couple of times. A click track could even be created that alternated between the meter change with and without the tempo change.

Whatever helps! Build your own metronome. Practice parts are meant to be changed in personal and unique ways. It's all about understanding what is needed to be able to play the music accurately and beautifully.

Re-notations

For many different reasons, the notated music that students see may not be the most understandable—it may not make sense or is in some way confusing. There are many choices to be made when notating music. Composers and publishers are often thinking of the big picture when they write, focusing on theoretical concepts and how the overall piece will sound to the audience. Sometimes composers forget to consider how easy—or difficult—the written notation is to read for the individual performer.

Of course the theoretical rules are important, but a teacher's primary job is to help students perform the music with the most beautiful sound possible. There is no need to be locked into the notation as presented on the page. Rather, lock onto the sound, because that is what's ultimately important for the performer—and the audience. It doesn't usually matter how the notes are *visually* presented in the score; the audience doesn't see the score. It doesn't matter to the audience if we are playing in 3/8 or 3/4 or if a note is written as an F# or a G*b*. The notes simply need to sound beautiful and part of a line.

In the examples that follow, we will show various ways teachers can guide students through the process of re-notating musical notation. This process has the additional benefit of opening up discussions about the theoretical organization of music and deepening the students' understanding of the music.

Spacing

Entering music into a notation program changes the spacing between the notes and the staves—and sometimes this change will help the students' learning. For instance, proportional notation spaces the notes to reflect the underlying meter; half notes would be spaced further from the next note than eighth notes. Some notation software allows spacing to be change for easier reading.

What we're suggesting isn't a new idea. It is an editor's job to change the visual score, sometimes drastically from the original, adding their own interpretations through slurs, phrase markings, and so on. Teachers frequently recommend editions that are easier to read because of the additional spacing between notes and staves. The following three excerpts are examples from three different editions of Mozart's *Piano Sonata* K. 331, 1st movement. Notice differences in spacing between the notes. In Figure 4.6, the notes are very close together.

In the Schirmer edition (see Figure 4.7), the editor has added extra performance instructions such as dynamics, articulations, and fingerings. Rhythmic spacing is proportional, which means that rhythms are spread out to visually represent their length.[6]

FIGURE 4.6 First edition of Mozart's *Piano Sonata No. 11 in A major*, K. 331, 1st movement, (measures 1–4), published by Artaria ca. 1784.

FIGURE 4.7 Schirmer edition of Mozart's *Piano Sonata No. 11 in A major*, K. 331, 1st movement, (measures 1–4), published 1893, edited by Lebert and Scharfenberg.

FIGURE 4.8 Henle edition of Mozart's *Piano Sonata No. 11 in A major*, K. 331, 1st movement, (measures 1–4), published 1977, edited by Seiffert and Bellheim.

The Henle edition in Figure 4.8 has extra separation between staves and only adds a few fingerings in a very small font, which adds a lot of visual space to the notation. Of these three editions, many pianists would find the Henle example easiest to read—yet the actual notes and rhythms of the piece have not changed.

Notation has never been static. The fact that various editions exist shows how flexible visual notation has always been. With today's technology, each performer can be their own editor.

Meter and rhythm

Notation programs allow students to change metric and rhythmic features, such as bar lines and beams, if it visually clarifies the music. Performers often have personal preferences for more or fewer notes under a beam. Some students would rather read eighth note patterns than sixteenth or thirty-second notes.

For instance, there may be a good theoretical reason why Beethoven wrote the second movement of his fifth symphony in 3/8 time with the eighth note at 92, but the extra beams may be visually confusing or distracting. The passage can easily be re-notated (see Figure 4.9), making it visually easier to understand. In a practice part, students are free to change the meter—augmenting the rhythm if that makes more visual sense.

Don't panic! This doesn't slow down the piece (the pulse will remain at 92 regardless of the note value of the pulse); it just visually changes how the notes look on the page. The goal is for ease of learning. It would be expected that the student would return to the original notation for performance.

Augmenting rhythms within pedagogical pieces has been common practice for many years, creating "simplified" versions or notational arrangements. For example, Beethoven's *Für Elise* has been frequently re-notated with augmented rhythms.[7]

Modern music can be particularly difficult, especially if it includes mixed or changing meter. Adding beams or augmenting the rhythm can help students see where patterns lie. Ades wrote figure 4.10 in 7/8. The second example re-notates the 7/8-meter into bars of 3/8 and 4/8. For many students, this example is simpler to read because the patterns are easier to see and there are smaller chunks to absorb. The last example

FIGURE 4.9 Excerpt of measures 81–82 of the violin I part of Beethoven's *Symphony No. 5*, 2nd movement, showing the original notation (example A). The rhythms were augmented in a notation program for easier reading changing the time signature to 3/4 (example B) and 3/2 (example C).

a) Original part entered into software program

b) Re-notated meter 3/8 + 4/8 alternating

c) Re-notated with augmented rhythm in 7/4

FIGURE 4.10 Excerpt of measures 1–6 of the bassoon part of Ades's *In Seven Days*, 5th movement, showing original part entered into a music notation program (example A), re-notated meter alternating 3/8 and 4/8 (example B), and re-notated meter augmenting the time signature to 7/4 (example C).

augments the rhythm and changes the meter to 7/4. This makes the rhythm easier to read by taking out most of the beams. Note that even though the meter and bar lines have changed, the sound remains the same in all examples.

While we're talking about rhythm, let's talk about beaming. Beams are in notation simply to help the performer visually group the stream of notes. Sometimes there are conventions or underlying reasons to beam in certain ways (usually beaming reflects meter), but that doesn't mean the student has to leave the beams as originally notated. Teachers can help students re-beam a passage to emphasize phrasing or patterns—maybe even re-beaming the passage multiple times—each time moving closer toward the original notation.

FIGURE 4.11 Excerpt of measures 25–27 of Chopin's *Nocturne, Op. 15, No. 2*, showing complex beaming in the top stave.

FIGURE 4.12 Excerpt of the top stave of measures 25–27 of Chopin's *Nocturne, Op. 15, No. 2*, re-notated in a music software program to simplify beaming.

> **BOX 4.8 Visit the companion website**
>
> ▶ Go to the companion website 4.6 to hear the original compared with this re-notated excerpt from *Chopin Nocturne, Op. 15*.

Figure 4.11, Chopin's *Nocturne*, Op. 15, No. 2 has very complicated beaming. There is a good reason why Chopin has notated the music in this way; the beams indicate inner voicing. However, the passage looks very difficult in the original notation.

When initially learning this passage, it might be beneficial to simplify the beaming in the right-hand stave to understand the basic outline. In the following example, the right-hand top fingerings were retained to help visually emphasize the upper melodic notes. It became immediately clear after the simplification, that the right hand has very easy octave movements and the passage is not that technically difficult to play. Re-notating a few measures changes the understanding of the piece so that the student realizes how simple it really is to perform (see Figure 4.12).

Key signatures and enharmonics

Musicians learn early that there are different ways to notate a pitch. The pitch C can be enharmonically rewritten as a B# or a D*bb*. The sound is the same.[8] The choice is obvious when composers are writing within a key, but when writing in modal, extended, or modulating harmonies, composers make decisions on how to notate a pitch and whether to use key signatures or add accidentals when necessary.

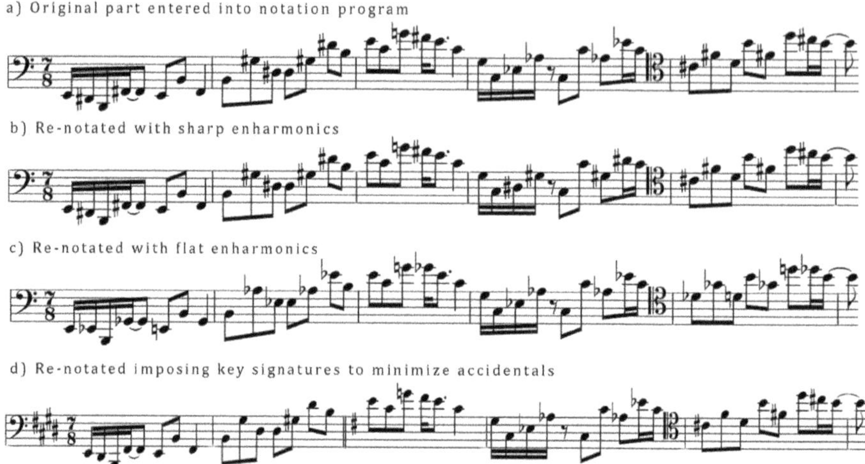

FIGURE 4.13 Excerpt of measures 1–6 of the bassoon part of Ades's *In Seven Days*, 5th movement, showing the original part entered into a music notation program (example A), re-notated with sharp enharmonics (example B), re-notated with flat enharmonics (example C), and re-notated imposing key signature to minimize accidentals (example D).

If the composer used notation that is in some way confusing, teachers can guide students in re-notating the pitch enharmonically or adding or removing a key signature. This may make all the difference to how easy the music is to learn. This is *especially* the case where a composer has chosen to mix flats and sharps. There maybe a theoretical reason to mix sharps and flats, but for the performer, switching accidentals can be confusing. In Figure 4.13, Ades has chosen to mix sharps and flats. The passage can easily be re-notated to reflect either flats or sharp enharmonics—whichever the performer finds easier to read. A student could even impose a key onto the passage for visual simplification of the accidentals.

In practice parts, performers decide which is better—using a key signature or accidentals—and not the composer.

Double sharps and flats can be especially problematic to read. In Figure 4.14, the accompaniment part for one of Reger's clarinet sonatas, the key of F# major is further complicated by the addition of double sharps and even a triple sharp (second bar, first beat, alto voice)! For practice, re-notating these measures into the simplest version of the notes can help expedite learning.

It's important to remember that in all the re-notated examples above, the sound has not changed, only the visual look of the music.

Clefs and ledger lines

Musicians who play in extreme ranges such as flautists may be used to reading large number of ledger lines, but for most performers, excessive ledger lines are confusing. Clefs such as alto or tenor and octave signs are tools composers use to keep pitches within the staff, making the music easier to read.

a) Original accompaniment part

b) Re-notation with enharmonics

FIGURE 4.14 Excerpt of measures 72–73 of the accompaniment part for Reger's *Clarinet Sonata, Op. 49 No. 2*, 4th movement (example A), and a re-notation created in a music notation program replacing the double and triple sharps with enharmonic equivalents (example B).

There are different conventions concerning clefs, depending on the instrument. Low strings, for instance, use multiple clefs such as treble, tenor, and bass to avoid ledger lines. Pianist may instead use 8va or 8ba to avoid ledger lines in lengthy high or low passages. Musicians become familiar with the conventions of their instruments, but if confronted with a piece that falls outside those conventions, learning becomes more difficult and takes more time. Re-notating a passage to match instrument conventions or a personal preference can make learning the music much more efficient.

Figure 4.15 is an excerpt from the bass part to Schoenberg's *Erwartung*. The original notation uses tenor and bass clefs. However, in the re-notation, Orin O'Brien preferred to read treble over tenor clef.[9]

Figure 4.16 is an example where reading 8va might be preferable to reading ledger lines. The first example is the original piano score, written with an abundant use of ledger lines. The composer was likely concerned with the left and right hands being very close together in the treble clef. Note that the original and the re-notation are the exact eight measures of music, but the re-notation looks much simpler and easier for students to sight read. The same passage can be further simplified by re-notating the double sharps.

These examples highlight how slight adjustments to the visual notation make passages easier to read for students. Try sight reading Examples A and C back to back—this may be a surprising experience for students!

A practice part gives teachers and students the freedom to explore the music visually rather than simply accepting the notation printed on the page. Notation software has

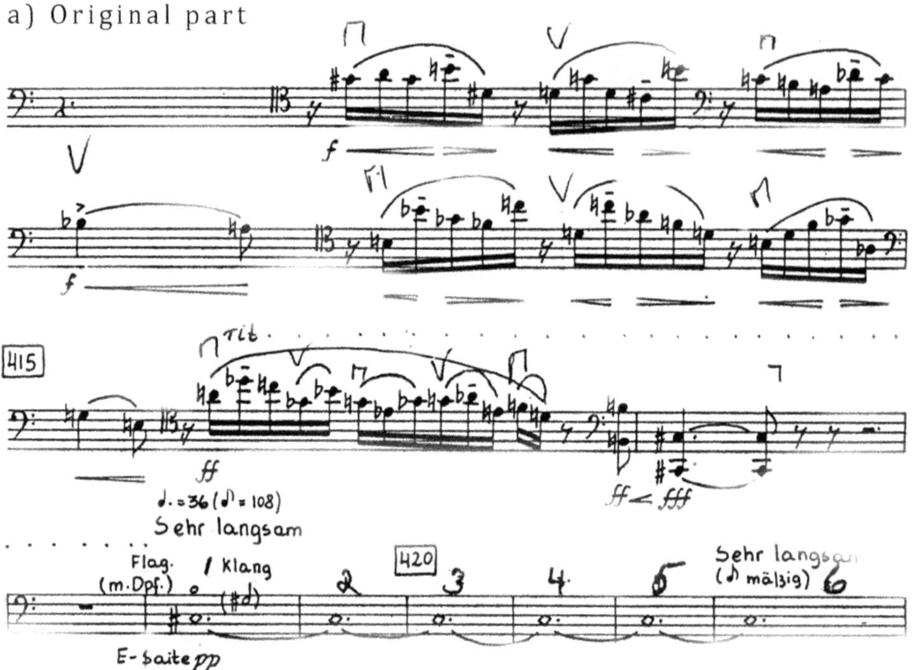

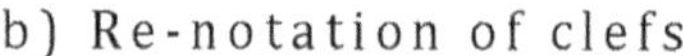

FIGURE 4.15 Excerpt of measures 413–424 of the bass part of Schoenberg's *Erwartung*, showing original notation (example A) and re-notated version created in a music notation program using treble and bass clefs (example B). Example B is based on a handwritten re-notation created by Orin O'Brien, bassist with the New York Philharmonic.

a) Original score

b) Re-notation using 8va

c) Re-notation enharmonic equivalents

FIGURE 4.16 Excerpt of measures 36–41 of Grieg's *Lyric Piece Op.57, No. 6*, showing the original score (example A), a re-notated version using 8vas created in a music notation program (example B), and a re-notation that further simplifies the example by using enharmonic equivalents (example C).

become simpler, and can now be used as a pedagogical tool. Teachers can guide students in finding and re-notating awkward passages in a different way—a way that makes personal sense.

Putting it all together

Figure 4.17 is a good summary of the ideas discussed in this chapter. The example is a melismatic passage representing one half of one measure of the piece *Litanies* by Marilyn Shrude. It is written with extensive ledger lines and an absence of bar lines.

The pianist found this passage difficult to learn, especially when reading notes with extensive ledger lines. The first step was to write in note names (see Figure 4.18).

However, this is a case where writing in note names wasn't enough. A re-notation of the score was needed to allow for faster learning: 8vas were added almost immediately to remove the extensive ledger lines (see Figure 4.19).

Meter, with corresponding bar lines and beams, was added to impose an organization on the melismatic passage (see Figure 4.20). This helped the performer perceive units in the music.

Next, it was helpful to standardize the accidentals (the original mixes sharps and flats). This particular musician preferred to read the example in all flats (see Figure 4.21).

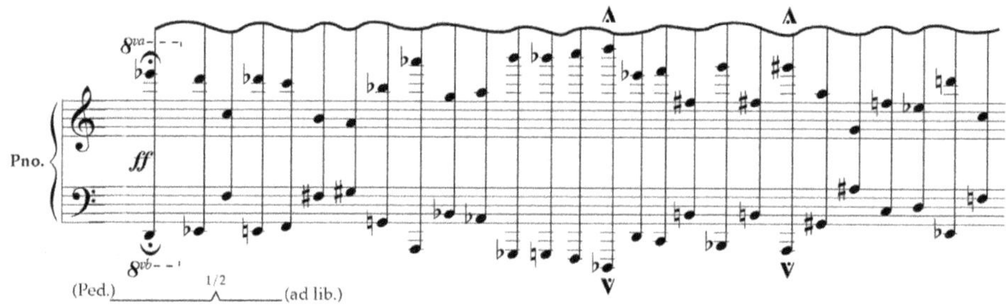

FIGURE 4.17 An excerpt (measure 66, first half) from the piano part of Marilyn Shrude's *Litanies*, originally scored for piano, flute, and oboe.

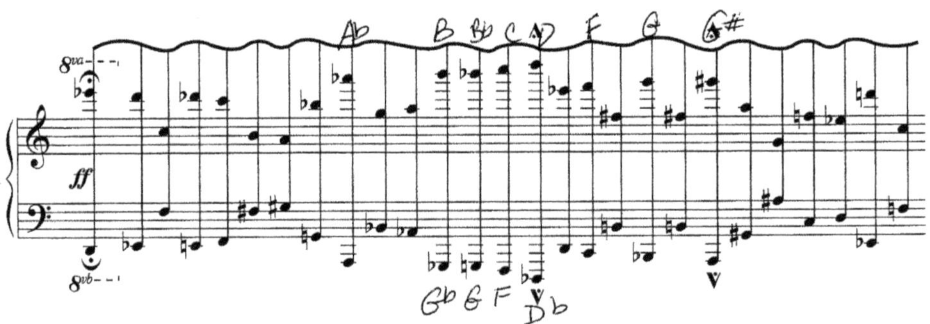

FIGURE 4.18 An excerpt (measure 66, first half) from the piano part of Marilyn Shrude's *Litanies*, originally scored for piano, flute, and oboe with handwritten note names written into the score.

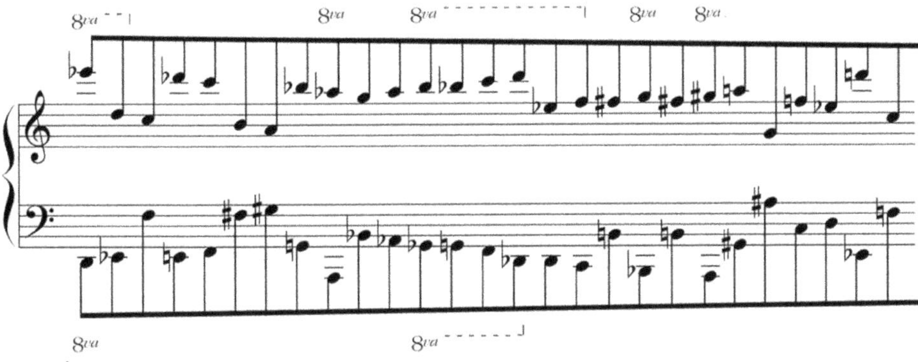

FIGURE 4.19 An excerpt (measure 66, first half) from the piano part of Marilyn Shrude's *Litanies* entered into a music notation program adding 8vas to remove extreme ledger lines.

FIGURE 4.20 An excerpt (measure 66, first half) from the piano part of Marilyn Shrude's *Litanies* entered into a music notation program adding 8vas and adding 4/8 meter with bar lines and beams.

FIGURE 4.21 An excerpt (measure 66, first half) from the piano part of Marilyn Shrude's *Litanies* entered into a music notation program adding 8vas, meter, and standardizing accidentals to favor flats.

Finally, spacing was altered to spread apart the eighth notes for easier reading (see Figure 4.22).

A performer could choose to change only one aspect of the passage or multiple aspects until the passage feels easier. The goal is to simply make the notation visually more accessible during practicing for faster learning.

FIGURE 4.22 An excerpt (measure 66, first half) from the piano part of Marilyn Shrude's *Litanies* entered into a music notation program adding 8vas, meter, enharmonics, and increasing the spacing between notes.

Creativity in practice

Up until now, we have explored using music notation software to create practice parts that help students read and understand their music more efficiently. This practice strategy changes the look of the music while keeping the sound of the music the same. In this section, we will take this idea a step further by showing how notation software can be used to arrange the music in some way to advance musical learning, adding an element of creativity and composition in the practice room.

We'll discuss three ways of creatively approaching technically difficult musical passages: isolating elements, simplifying the music, and creating personalized etudes. Each of these strategies is firmly rooted in tried-and-true practice strategies, but music notation software elevates and extends the practice possibilities.

Isolating elements

If a musical passage is especially difficult, practice may need to start with isolating elements like practicing rhythm without pitch or playing pitches without rhythm. Even singing a part is a form of isolating elements. This strategy strips away the some of the technical requirements needed to produce the music and allows the student to focus on the remaining features of the music.

Students often forget about this practice strategy and opt to instead practice everything at once—maybe at a slower tempo—but still practicing all the elements. Instead, simplifying and increasing complexity by increments may actually be the faster way to achieve the ultimate goal. We introduced the practice strategy of isolating musical elements in chapter 1.

Young musicians may struggle with this strategy because they aren't always able to isolate elements for practice in their heads in the same way experienced musicians can. It can be confusing for a musician to play something that is in some way different from what they see on the page. To help young musicians effectively use this practice strategy, music notation programs make it easy to visually isolate musical elements on the page so that the music notation matches what the student is playing.

In Figure 4.23, we return to the Martini *Gavotte* example for violin presented earlier in the book. It might be helpful for a young player to isolate the movements of the right arm (bow arm) by playing the rhythm on an open string (example B), then adding the slurs and other articulations (example C), and finally adding the string crossings still without fingerings (example D). After the rhythm and bow arm technique is solidified, students can then isolate the melodic line (example E).

FIGURE 4.23 Notation for measures 1–4 of Martini's *Gavotte*, showing the original created in a notation program (example A), the rhythm isolated on an open string (example B), the rhythm with articulations (example C), the rhythm with articulations and string crossings (example D), and the melodic notes isolated (example E).

Simplifying the music

Music notation software can also be used to simplify the music. By simplifying, we mean temporarily removing notes or restructuring the music in some way to make it easier to learn. In other words, making an arrangement of the piece. We are focusing our discussion on younger players, but all musicians can benefit from visually reducing the complexity of the piece to understand the underlying structure.

Simplifying melodies is also an important strategy for ensemble directors when working with students of varying abilities. Less able students can successfully play a simplified arrangement of the music with the group rather than struggling through the performance version, often bogging down the tempo or muddying the sound. These simplified arrangements can consist of chordal tones or key melodic pitches.

Often times the most complex music is actually very simple at heart.

Skeletal melodies

Simplifying a melody can be as easy as removing passing tones or reducing the melody to only a few key pitches—the skeleton of the melody. In a very complex passage, the important pitches may not be immediately obvious to the student. Providing students with a simplified melody—or better yet, asking students to find the key pitches—helps the student understand the music at a deeper level.

In chapter 1 we discussed blocking chords, which is an example of simplifying the music. Figure 4.24 shows how the left-hand alberti bass pattern may be simplified by blocking the chord changes (example B, bottom stave). Simplifying can be taken a step further by reducing the right-hand melodic notes to just the essential pitches, removing the written-out turn and ornaments (example B, top stave). This ensures that the student focuses on the pulse. Practicing this simplified version helps solidify the important melodic pitches in the student's ear.

It's important to practice the simplified version using fingerings and articulations that will transfer to the final performance version of the melody. When the simplified

FIGURE 4.24 Notation for measures 1–4 of Mozart's *Piano Sonata*, K. 545, 1st movement, showing the original score (example A) and simplified version (example B), with blocked chords in the left-hand (bottom stave) and simplified melodic line (top stave).

version fits well in the fingers, additional pitches may be added to increase complexity and move the simplified version incrementally toward the final performance version (for instance, adding the sixteenth note rhythms but not the trill). Eventually, the student can switch to playing the passage from the original score.

After all, much of the ensemble music performed with young children is already a simplified arrangement. Simplifying a version even further for a few students is simply another form of arranging. Figure 4.25 shows how a published arrangement simplified the original piece and how the passage can be further simplified. Ensemble directors may be able to anticipate which children will struggle with the concert music and have a simplified arrangement prepared in advance. Students may never even realize that they're playing an adapted version. Ensemble directors can create a new violin III part or a cello II part. Students can then feel that they are fully contributing to creating music with the entire group.

Earlier in the chapter, we explored creating an aural model using music notation software. Students can play their simplified versions along with these digital aural models. This helps students hear their final performance goal and ensures the simplified version keeps the character of the original piece. Students can also play a simplified version alongside a student playing from the original music to create a fun duet. Both students benefit from this activity. The student playing the simplified version hears the music in all its complexity, and the student playing the original hears the emphasis placed on the important underlying structure of the passage.

Sometimes a student's problem lies in visually tracking through the music without getting bogged down in details. If this is the case, excerpting the first beat of each bar in a notation program will help the students keep moving in tempo. When the performer

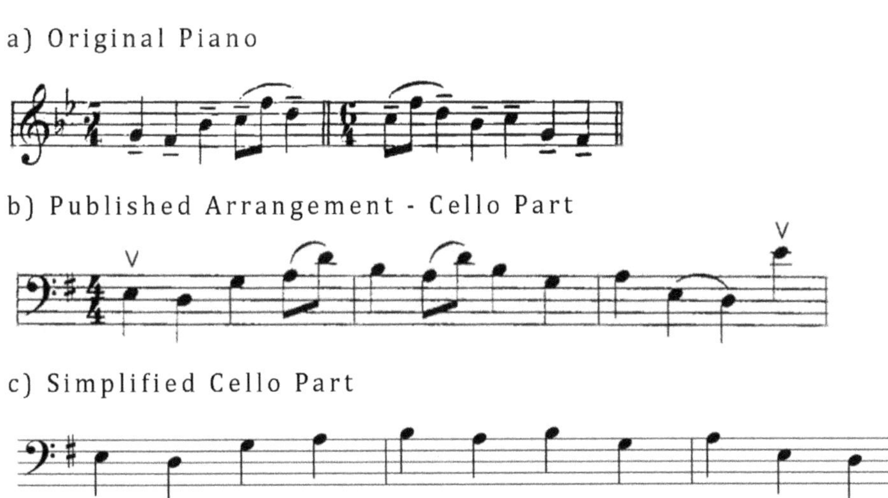

FIGURE 4.25 Excerpt of measures 1–2 of the original piano part of Mussorgsky's *Pictures at an Exhibition* (example A), showing how this passage was simplified by Jennifer Mishra for the published Alfred arrangement (example B) and how the passage could be further simplified (example C).

is comfortable, add another beat (e.g., beat 3 in 4/4 time). In this way, a piece is built up beat by beat.

Of course we want all of our students to be able to play every note on the page accurately and exactly as the composer wrote, but sometimes—for the sake of beautiful music—it's better to leave out a note or two and play the passage cleanly rather than try for all the notes.[10] Building a passage up from a simple version is much like building up the tempo using a metronome.

Redistributing parts

The idea of redistributing parts is primarily relevant for pianists, where the music is distributed between left and right hands, but ensemble performers may also find this practice strategy relevant when playing *divisi*. Pianists sometimes find that changing left-hand notes to the right hand (or visa versa) facilitates better voicing or a more fluent technique. There are various opinions about this practice. Some performers feel strongly that the music should be played exactly the way it was written by the composer, including how the notes were distributed between the hands. Other performers feel equally strongly that it doesn't matter what hand plays the notes as long as the musical product is what the composer intended.

Redistributing notes between the hands does not necessarily require re-notating the music, though this can help visually simplify the score for learning. Dallas Weekley and Nancy Arganbright, the renowned piano duet team, publishes their own editions with parts redistributed and describe the process beautifully in their book *The Piano Duet: A Learning Guide* excerpted in Box 4.9.[11]

The idea of redistribution of parts can be extended to *create* duets from solo works. In essence, dividing one part into two. This is not a new idea. Brahms himself arranged

BOX 4.9 From the performers

Even the best composers seem to be oblivious to the problems they create by writing the same notes for two players, or causing overlapping hand positions. Did they compose by sliding back and forth on a bench from primo to secondo positions? Did they neglect to examine the hand positions carefully while playing with a partner?

It becomes obvious, then, that we must use common sense to correct such awkward passages while maintaining the integrity of the notes and related aspects of the musical content. In other words, the adjustments we make in how the music is played should not alter how the music sounds.

—Dallas Weekley and Nancy Arganbright, piano duettists[12]

various versions of his *Waltzes, Op. 39*. The original version was written for four-hand duet, which Brahms arranged for two pianos, solo piano, and even published a simplified version (see Figure 4.26).

It's important not to underestimate student potential, but for some students, confidently performing a simplified version might be their successful level of performance. For other students, these simplified versions are only stepping stones toward the original notation.

FIGURE 4.26 Excerpt of measures 1–4 of Brahms's *Waltz Op. 39, No. 15*, showing the two piano version (example A), the solo version in A*b* (example B), and the simplified version in A major (example C).

The etude-ist

Sometimes a musical passage just defies learning. Instead of coming to the passage again and again and being frustrated at the lack of improvement, approach the problem from a more creative direction. Compose a personal etude, going beyond the printed notes.

Etudes are simply exercises created to target a specific technical challenge. There are many published etudes (e.g., Kreisler, Czerny), but every piece has unique problems and there may not be an etude to help. Using music notation programs, students can compose their own technical exercises. Sometimes student-created etudes are actually more difficult than the original technical challenge, after which coming back to the original passage seems much easier.

The first step is to really zoom in and identify the technical problem in question. Is it a difficulty with a string crossing, an awkward fingering, or a challenging leap? Targeting the technical issue, students vary the music in creative ways, such as changing the rhythm or imposing accents. Have fun with this step! Play the passage backward, turn it upside down. Creating etudes is all about playing with the music to approach the technical problem from every possible angle. Students may come up with ideas that the teacher would never have thought of (see Figure 4.27).

FIGURE 4.27 Excerpt of measures 25–27 of Del Borgo's *Suite for Strings*, showing the start of a difficult fugue passage created in a notation program (example A) and possible variations of the passage (examples B–F).

Finally, it's time to string together the best variations into a unique etude. There are no rules to creating these personal etudes, and some variations will work better than others. Sequencing and repetition are great compositional devices to use when composing the etude.

Creating these etudes is a great way of targeting a technical difficulty, and if used in an ensemble setting, can address compositional teaching standards.[13] Students can continue to use their personal etudes as warm-ups—or even swap exercises with students learning the same piece.

Conclusion

This chapter has focused on notation software as a pedagogical tool to enhance student performance. This tool is probably best used when other practice strategies have failed—in those difficult passages where nothing else seems to work.

Practice parts are re-notations of the original piece, keeping the sound of the music while simplifying the visual look of the notation. They are personal and subjective. What makes sense to one student visually may not make sense to another. That's fine! Practice parts allow the performer the freedom to favor his or her own visual preferences, rather than the composer's. Practice parts make the music visually easier to read and ultimately easier to learn.

Musical notation software also allows the teacher and student to approach the printed music creatively, tackling problem passages with innovative, and original solutions. Creating arrangements that isolate elements, simplifying passages, or devising new etudes deconstructs the music in a way that enhances learning.

We're all after the same thing—beautiful music.

Notes

1. Information about Finale (and their free version Notepad) may be found at www.finalemusic.com. MuseScore may be downloaded at https://musescore.org and Noteflight may be accessed at www.noteflight.com.
2. Musical notation has evolved significantly over the centuries. For an overview of the history of notation see Thomas Forrest Kelly's book *Capturing Music*, and for a scholarly look into how musical notation and performance practice interact see Roberto Poli's book *The Secret Life of Musical Notation*.
3. The quote from Arlen Fast was published as part of a research study by Jennifer Mishra and Barbara Fast in their article "Practising in the New World."
4. Musicologist Julia Ronge wrote this quote to explain Beethoven's manuscript copied from Mozart's *Quartett für zwei Violinen, Viola und Violoncello* (G-Dur) KV 387, Partitur. The manuscript may be seen in the Beethoven-Haus Bonn Digital Archives at www.beethoven.de/sixcms/detail.php?id=15288&template=dokseite_digitales_archiv_en&_dokid=wm99&_seite=1-1.
5. Information about the Amazing Slow Downer may be found at www.ronimusic.com.
6. Readers interested in exploring spacing in musical notation more fully should reference John Sloboda's article "The Uses of Space in Music Notation."
7. An example of a simplified version of *Für Elise* is edited by James Bastien and published by Neil A. Kjos Music.

8. The sound of enharmonically re-spelled notes will be the same on keyboard instruments, though possibly shaded differently depending on key and chord tone within an ensemble.
9. A handwritten re-notation of *Erwartung* was created by Orin O'Brien, bassist with New York Philharmonic, and shared with the authors as part of an unpublished research study titled "An Exploration of Practicing Strategies Related to the Premiere of Classical Music."
10. Arlen Fast, bassoonist in the New York Philharmonic, talks about leaving out isolated notes for the overall effect of the music in the article by Jennifer Mishra and Barbara Fast "Practising in the New World."
11. The piano duet team of Weekley and Arganbright has published a ten-volume series of their editions of piano duets with many examples of redistributed parts. For more information, visit their website at http://weekleyarganbright.com/music-books.
12. The quote may be found on page 15 of the book *The Piano Duet* by Dallas Weekley and Nancy Arganbright.
13. Information about the 2014 music standards developed by the National Association for Music Education (NAfME) may be found at https://nafme.org/my-classroom/standards/core-music-standards.

5

Beyond Four Walls

Practicing as a Social Activity

Introduction

This chapter is all about leveraging social media to help students become better musicians. Most students use social media in their daily lives, but not necessarily in their musical lives. With today's technology, musical learning can expand beyond the four walls of a studio or practice room. Used well, technology can help eliminate the isolation of traditional music practice and bring music students closer together.

Most activities in a child's life are social (e.g., sports, dance, martial arts), including many of their classroom activities. Even when a school activity appears isolated, such as completing a math worksheet, it is completed alongside other children working on the same activity. There is a camaraderie even if the activity is not overtly collaborative.

Musical practice is starkly different.

Private music lessons are traditionally designed in a one-on-one model where students primarily interact with one private instructor followed by isolated practice. School ensembles provide a social component in music, but home practice is typically solitary. Many students love to participate in ensembles, but then find they do not have the same motivation to practice at home.

As the music student matures, more and more time is expected to be devoted to isolated practice. Some children adapt well and find that they can concentrate more fully when alone. However, many people (adults and children alike) are not comfortable with being alone and become passive and lonely.[1] For some adolescents, being alone can lead to negative mood states.[2] This is not to say that being alone is necessarily a negative experience, but it is important to recognize that many people struggle with solitary activities. Some children may be so uncomfortable working by themselves that they may choose to abandon music completely.

In this chapter we advocate increasing social interaction through practice partners—but don't worry if these types of social partner activities don't work for all students. Some students work fine alone. The activities discussed in this chapter are for motivating the *other* students who may not find solitary practice easy.

One is a lonely number

The idea that children learn best when working in a social environment is not new. Social constructivism was pioneered by educator Lev Vygotsky, and emphasizes learning through social interactions. Central to this educational theory is that people tend to learn best in groups where there is a sense of camaraderie, as well as responsibility. Furthermore, children learn both from teachers and peers ("more knowledgeable others"), and learn best by interacting in some way with the information they are learning.[3]

Teachers use a variety of methods to make individual lessons more social. Scheduling studio classes is one way students can share their musical experiences and avoid the isolation of private lessons. This is particularly helpful for students playing instruments such as piano that are learned completely outside of the ensemble environment. Including parents is another way of making music lessons a more collaborative, shared experience. For instance, the Suzuki method provides a model for integrating parents into the lesson. Parents become a motivating, built-in home practice companion.

Teachers can also set up practice partners—students who practice together some of the time. These practice sessions can be short, and don't necessarily replace daily practice. The sessions can be fun and at least the students get to the practice room. Partners can self-select or be paired by the teacher (for instance, a weak student with a strong student). A teacher may wish to assign specific practice activities, since some lend themselves better to social practicing, specifically those that students tend to put off such as scales or technique-building exercises. A practice "date" with a peer may be the motivation needed to tackle the activity. Practice partners also provide an audience for each other and can give helpful feedback.

Leveraging social media

This chapter is about exploring the use of technology to make musical practice more social and motivating. We'll begin by exploring how technology can be used to make practice into a game. Digital activity tracking apps (useful in tracking exercise, etc.) come in all shapes and sizes, from simple rep counters to elaborate virtual reality games. One thing they all have in common is their ability to motivate students to practice more and more often. The score and reward systems built into these types of programs gamifies practice—making practice as addictive as playing video games. The sharing feature on these apps adds a level of social competitiveness that, used thoughtfully, adds yet another level of motivation.

Continuing with the topic of social media, we'll present ideas that extend the possibilities for learning and practicing using social media. Using common technology, students can connect with each other about their practicing—and even use features already built into the programs to virtually interact in real time. Platforms constantly change, with new formats emerging every year (e.g., Instagram, Snapseed). Practice strategies can easily be adapted, and innovative ideas will emerge with new platforms.

Online distance education has been a major topic for decades, especially in higher education. The digital format has made long-distance education much more accessible, though it has not replaced traditional in-person teaching and learning. We'll explore Skype and FaceTime as platforms that can connect students together as practice partners, but of course teachers and students can also connect using these same platforms. This section is all about teaching music at a distance—whether the distance be from halfway around the world or the next street over.

Sometimes the hardest part about practicing is getting started. So, let's jump right in!

MyPracticePal: digital activity trackers

Getting started is the biggest hurdle for many activities that people don't want to do, such as exercising, tracking calories, and—let's face it—practicing. For some people, practicing is simply not their favorite thing to do. They may love performing and the social aspect of making music, but practicing can be a chore. Digital activity trackers motivate students to practice and make practicing social, virtually interacting with others who are doing the same activity.

Timing apps like Toggl or ATracker or music specific apps like ProMusica are the next generation of practice logs.[4] The 21st century has moved well beyond documenting practice time with paper and pencil ("practice cards"). Today's digital activity trackers are useable, fun, and provide feedback to the student. Flexible activity trackers like Toggl allow students to easily set up and time tasks within a practice session, moving the timer easily from one activity to another with a push of a button. This app also quickly shows how practice was distributed throughout the day or week. Even devices like Fitbit and apps such as MyFitnessPal can log practicing—after all, practicing *is* exercise (one hour of practicing can burn between 100–200 calories!).[5]

Tracking practice time creates a motivational goal and almost a sense of urgency, and practicing becomes more focused when a timer sets the boundaries. There's a reason why tracking time in activities such as exercise is very popular in today's culture. Time

BOX 5.1 Visit the companion website

▶ Visit the companion website 5.1 for a review of some of our favorite apps useful for timing practice and tracking practice goals.

becomes a type of "score," a number we love to beat (that's why video games can become so addictive).

The fact is that tracking practice increases practice time.[6] Having a specific goal, whether it is amount of time (e.g., ten minutes on scales) or number of days (e.g., practice etudes five days a week), creates self-accountability. It's helpful for teachers to be clear about their expectations, and in many instances teachers and students can work together to set up a practice schedule.[7] With today's technology, students and teachers can easily see if goals are being met. In Box 5.2, Lance Drege describes why he uses Toggl in his percussion studio.

Some teachers create studio- or class-wide practice competitions based on daily practice. This type of social competition exists in many aspects of our lives. For instance, motivational tracking is built into daily online experiences, everything from sharing exercise goals on Facebook through apps like MyFitnessPal to earning badges as a reviewer for TripAdvisor.[8] Digital trackers like Toggl can be setup to include an element of social competition.

Both music-specific and general activity trackers allow students to automatically track practice time. But it's not just about simply tracking time; it's about using our practice time well. In the following sections, we'll explore various ways of using digital activity trackers to make practicing more focused and efficient.

BOX 5.2 From a performer and teacher

The Toggl app was really designed for business as a billing app. But it had everything I needed for tracking practice time: it was free, cross-platform, could be used on any computer or phone, students could create as many projects as they wanted. They could invite me to see their projects. In percussion we have to study multiple instruments, and we'll spend half a lesson on snare drum, half a lesson on marimba, for instance. I wanted them to see that they were devoting equal time to each instrument. I've always been a proponent of setting goals. It has shown them where they are practicing; are they practicing too much on some pieces [and] not others? If they were having issues with their lesson, or juries, I could go into their report and say, "Look, your practicing the last two weeks is different than it was before." After juries I sat down with each student and went through their toggle time and goals, and those who met their performance goals, actually met their practice goals. And those who didn't meet their performance goals, also didn't meet their practice goals. It's given me a lot of insight and has helped my students monitor their time.

—Lance Drege, percussion professor, University of Oklahoma

Just do it!: getting started

Sometimes it's not about the total amount of time a student practices—it's about getting the student to the practice room. Timers work well as initial motivating tools. They help us get started. An hour of practice can seem overwhelming, but a 15- to 20-minute goal seems do-able. Success: twenty minutes have quickly passed, so let's keep going!

Currently popular is the Pomodoro technique created by Francesco Cirillo.[9] "Pomodoro" means "tomato" in Italian, and was developed based on a common kitchen timer shaped like a tomato (for an app version of a pomodoro timer see Figure 5.1). Central to this time management method is breaking tasks into twenty-five-minute segments and then taking a rewarding five-minute break. The goal is to complete a certain number of "pomodoros" in a day (e.g., four to eight). This technique encourages focusing on one activity at a time. Because the pomodoros are short, it's easy to get started. In terms of musical practice, students can do "musical tomatoes"—short, twenty-minute practice segments interspersed with a five-minute break. This emphasizes distributed over massed practice—and even interleaving practice, topics explored in chapter 1.

Any digital tracking apps can help students organize short practice sessions, but there are many pomodoro-specific apps like Tomato One.[10] These are setup for short

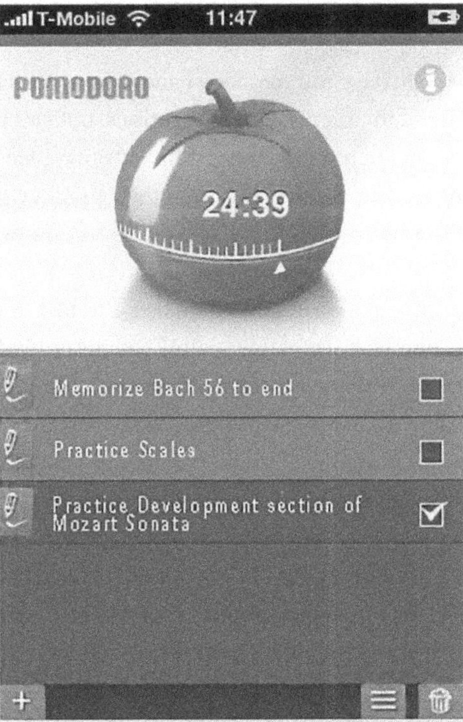

FIGURE 5.1 This screenshot of the app Pomodoro Time Management shows the tomato-shaped timer, which is the basis of the Pomodoro technique, and allows the user to specify a list of tasks to be completed during the twenty-five-minute time.

twenty- to twenty-five-minute blocks of activity with built-in breaks. Pomodoro apps generally count down from twenty or twenty-five minutes. This tends to be more satisfying than timers that count up.

For children, it can be fun to set a random amount of time each day to practice, rather than a fixed twenty minutes. Times like 17.5 minutes or 22 and 1/3 minutes are more "fun" numbers than "twenty." Randomizer apps like Decide, Now! let teachers or parents enter a list of practice times, and students can spin the dial to find out how much time they get to practice today.[11] Music is fun, and once students start they often get in the flow and end up practicing more than the set time.

Up to this point, we've been talking about practicing as one task, but in reality practicing breaks down into many different parts (scales, sight reading, segments of repertoire, etc.). In the next section, we'll show how each element of practicing can be its own task. Combining these tasks together creates a practice routine.

Virtual practice trainer: setting practice routines

Practice sessions can be thought of like exercise routines. Both start with warm-ups (scales, long tones, etc.) and often include strength training (woodshedding and etudes), intensive cardio (longer play-through and endurance playing), and cool-downs (fun play-throughs reviews). Even the popular interval training in exercise (where activities requiring different speeds, effort, etc. are alternated) can equate to interleaving practice, discussed in chapter 1.

Students don't always have good memories about how they've managed their practice time. They might intend to practice difficult sections, but end up focusing on the easy passages.[12] Even experts can fall into this trap.[13] Students may also practice at times when they are tired or inattentive. They sometimes cram their practice rather than distributing it over time. Practicing five hours on the day before a lesson is not the same as practicing one hour a day over five days.[14]

Breaking practice into smaller segments makes the task much more specific and attainable. Rather than one task, "practice violin," create individual tasks for different aspects of daily practice such as scales, segments of repertoire, and technique-building exercise. "Practice B*b* major scale for five minutes" is more specific than "practice scales." Building a practice routine consisting of smaller attainable tasks is much more motivating than an ill-defined practice goal.

Programmable timers that can alternate between activities help keep practice routines on track. For instance, Interval Timer has an elegant interface and can be programed to sound alarms at various points in practice to signal a move to another activity.[15] This app also has tracking data to show which days the students have practiced and provides a graph of their practicing on each day. The ProMusica app tracks time on specific musical goals ("issue tracker"), including ideal metronome markings.[16] The program allows students to record practicing directly into the app. When the goal is achieved, it can be satisfyingly checked off.

When setting up a programmable timer, use the "rule of 10s"—each activity is practiced for ten minutes (this can be modified to the "rule of 5s" for younger children or the "rule of 20s" for more advanced musicians):[17]

- 10 minutes of warm-up
- 10 minutes practicing etude
- 10 minutes of scales
- 10 minutes practicing Beethoven *Sonata*, etc.

Alternatively, teachers can set up a personalized practice routine for each student depending on repertoire requirements.

- 5 minutes of warm-up
- 10 minutes practicing etude
- 7 minutes of scales
- 15 minutes practicing Beethoven *Sonata*, etc.

With technology, teachers can even check in during the week and intervene if practice is going awry. Programs like Collabra and iScore time students' practice through videos uploaded or recorded directly into the program.[18] Teachers can drop in on students' practicing during the week to see exactly what they are doing during practice time. Even watching five to ten minutes of a practice session can reveal how effectively—or ineffectively—the student is using practice time. Teachers can even correct the errors or provide encouragement midweek by commenting on the video.

If a student is not progressing in their lessons, than looking at practice times and distribution over the course of a couple of weeks may reveal a pattern. A visual graph of time distribution, like the one generated in Toggl for Figure 5.2, can be very powerful.

Burst mode

Timing techniques are particularly useful when tackling difficult sections with focused attention. "Burst mode" is a strategy that alternates practicing multiple short sections for brief amounts of time.[19] This is a quick-fire practice technique that helps when woodshedding tricky passages.

When using burst mode, divide the piece into short, technically challenging sections. Then, set a basic repeating timer (also known as an "interval timer") to loop a three-minute or five-minute alarm. Each time the alarm sounds, quickly move to the next section. When all the passages have been practiced, go around again in the same order, backward, or even randomly—it doesn't matter! The important point is to return repeatedly to these difficult sections for short bursts of intensive practicing.

The burst mode technique takes advantage of the interleaving practice strategy we discussed in chapter 1. Returning to the material keeps the passage fresh and encourages

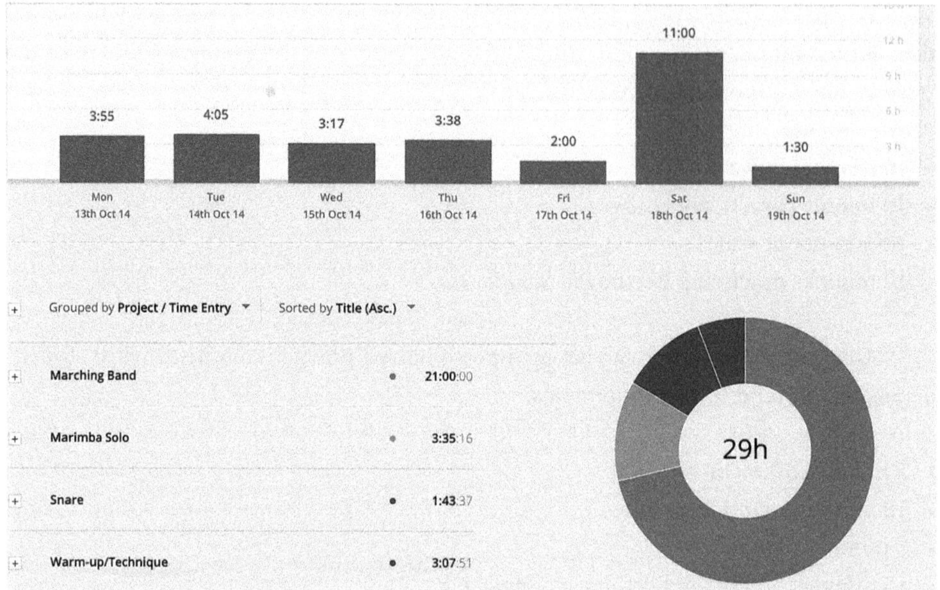

FIGURE 5.2 Screenshot of graphs created in the Toggl app showing distribution of practice time over the course of a week by an undergraduate percussion major.

focused practice. Though counterintuitive to most musicians, this strategy of practicing in short bursts is generally more efficient in the long run than an extended period of practice.

This strategy works particularly well with scales or other technical practice that isn't always the most enjoyable. "Super burst modes" (i.e., super-short bursts of time, such as nine seconds) interspersed throughout the practice session or a lesson adds motivation and an intensity to the practice that wouldn't normally accompany these activities—and it's fun!

Gamifying practice: counting and reward systems

Video games can be highly enjoyable—but also highly addictive. There's something in the score–reward system of most games that is compelling and keeps us coming back for more.

Gamifying music practice applies a system of scores and rewards to the practicing activity. Any "score" will do (time practiced, attempts played, or levels achieved), and rewards for completing tasks can be actual or virtual—making practice into a game. Students can often share their scores and accomplishments to add another level of social engagement to the practice game.

Gamifying practice can be as simple as counting repetitions. A familiar game for musicians is to play a passage perfectly three or five times in a row, moving candy or paperclips to the other side of the stand to keep track. An error sends you back to square

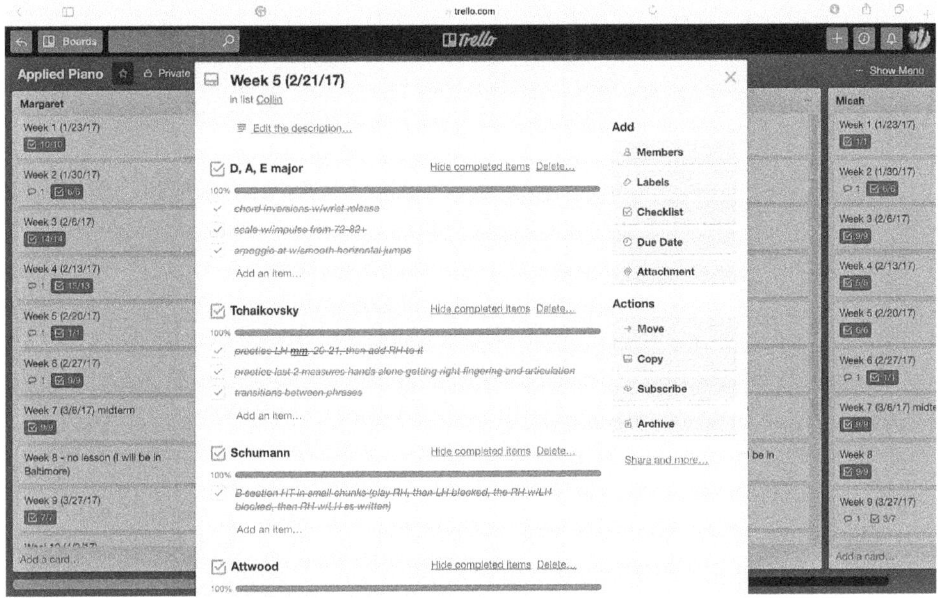

FIGURE 5.3 Screenshot of list of practicing tasks created in the Trello app by Jennifer Stadler for her piano studio.

one. A 21st-century version of this game uses counting apps, which are popular with athletes to keep track of reps. Apps like Bean Count, Counter, and Tally Counter are colorful and customizable for counting any activity, including a musical practice activity.[20]

Gamifying musical practice need not be complex. Even simple to-do list apps (e.g., Trello, Productive) will do the trick.[21] Scores are based on the number of musical tasks completed, whether the tasks be number of scales played at a certain tempo or amount of time devoted to a specific piece of music. To-do list apps also provide a virtual reward system—don't underestimate the satisfaction of checking off a completed task.[22] The apps that provide a visual graph, status bar, or numerical update to indicate progress toward a goal, are the most game-like and motivating (see Figure 5.3). Many to-do list apps also include timers or send daily alerts when it's time to practice (Toodledo).[23]

Practice Buddy is a music-specific app that gamifies practice. It is simple to set up practice goals (both in terms of time and specific achievements) and rewards for the students such as virtual stickers.[24] Teachers can use the app to monitor practice if they wish. Students record one minute of practicing to send to the teacher for feedback.

Familiar games like Jeopardy are now online and easily customizable for motivating practice (see Figure 5.4).[25] This type of game can include anything from scales to specific measures of repertoire. Potentially tedious activities suddenly become important to master to gain points in the game. This type of game works particularly well in group settings and adds to the competitiveness. Announcing that the game will happen during the next class period may be all that is needed to get students to the practice room!

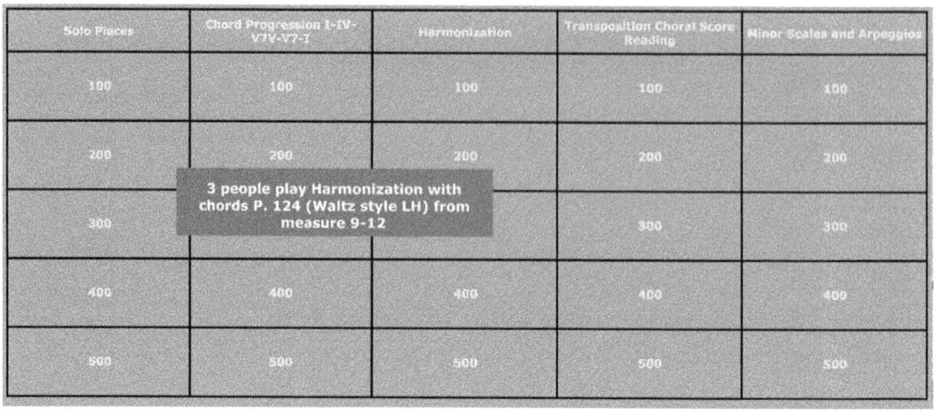

Solo Pieces	Chord Progression I-IV-V7V-V7-I	Harmonization	Transposition Choral Score Reading	Minor Scales and Arpeggios
100	100	100	100	100
200	200	200	200	200
300			300	300
400	400	400	400	400
500	500	500	500	500

3 people play Harmonization with chords P. 124 (Waltz style LH) from measure 9-12

FIGURE 5.4 Screenshot of an online Jeopardy game created by Chin Jung Hsieh for use in a university group piano class.

Online programs like Habitica create an elaborate virtual world infinitely customizable for music practice.[26] Students who are avid gamers or who like tracking other elements of their lives will connect with this format. Teachers assign practice tasks such as scales or sight reading, and can also set up group challenges where the students all work toward a common goal. This program gives virtual, gaming-style rewards when tasks are completed that can be customized by teachers and parents. Tasks can be set up to repeat daily, and skipping a day subtracts points from the total score.

Breaking practice down into manageable activities and gamifying these tasks makes practicing more motivating and exciting. Digital activity trackers help students keep to a set practice routine and keep track of breaks. These apps also provide virtual rewards, making practice feel satisfying—so the students are more likely to do it—especially if they share their accomplishments.

Sharing the love . . . of practicing

In this section, we're talking about leveraging social media platforms like Facebook, Instagram, YouTube, Snapchat, or Twitter to encourage students to practice more—and maybe even practice more attentively.[27] With social media, students no longer have to practice alone. Social media allows students to interact, sharing practice goals and accomplishments. Students become accountable to each other and may be motivated to accomplish more than the teacher expected. Feedback from peers comes from a different perspective, which adds to the richness of learning.

Any social media platform will work. Teachers should choose one that they find easy to use. Most students will buy into the teachers' excitement even if it's not the platform that they use every day. Be willing to explore and try out new platforms, but don't get caught up in chasing the newest technology. Remember, this is all about sharing the music.

Be prepared to teach students how to use important features in the chosen platform. Some students use social media more than others or may know only one or two platforms. Often peers can help each other figure out any technical issues that arise.

We recommend creating a dedicated space for a studio or classroom. This can be as easy as setting up a dedicated Facebook page or YouTube channel. The benefit is that student postings are all in one place and are kept separate from personal social media. Check privacy options carefully on each platform. Ideally, only students enrolled in a studio or class should be able to see the postings.

Each platform has useful features, and this section is about how to use these various features to improve practicing. For instance, at the time of writing this book, Instagram was popular. This platform allows users to upload photos, sixty seconds of video, and write mini-blog posts. Students can use these features to share aspects of their practicing and help them meet musical goals.

Instagram my practice

Social media is perfect for sharing selfies—both regular photo selfies and musical selfies. As discussed in chapter 3, musical selfies are self-recordings of daily practice or performance. Sharing these with fellow musicians directs extra attention onto practice and adds a slight feeling of performance to what is normally a behind-the-scenes activity. Students can interact with each other by giving "likes" (virtual pats-on-the-back) and helpful comments. These can inspire students to practice more.

An instant first step is to ask students to post photo selfies showing themselves practicing. These can be candid photos or a fun pose including the instrument and music (see Figure 5.5). Selfies are especially fun to create when practicing with a partner. These selfies show that the students got their instruments out, and that's the first step.

Musical selfies heighten the interest and interactivity between students. Musical selfies can be powerful social motivators. When students see their peers posting practice selfies, they are more likely to post themselves—which means practicing more! But students may need a prompt to help them choose an appropriate musical selfie to share. One prompt to get students started is "Show us your best." For instance:

- Show us your best scale.
- Show us your best performance.
- Show us your best articulation.
- Show us your best ten (seconds).

Teachers can highlight the practice selfies—especially the creative ones—on a studio website or Facebook page for additional motivation.

Sharing practice-performance videos with three to five friends can be particularly effective when preparing for recitals or concerts. It's not always easy to arrange a live audience to practice a performance, but social media makes it easy to arrange a virtual

FIGURE 5.5 Photo selfie of two university music majors during a partner practice session for a group piano class. Photo used by permission of Sarah Spurlin and Kyle Sutherland.

audience. Students could even share live videos using platforms like Facebook, Twitter, or Instagram stories.

But sharing is only one half of the learning experience; the other is giving helpful feedback to peers. The students motivate each other and quickly slip into the role of teacher—which they always love! Teaching solidifies and organizes knowledge, helping students to internalize their learning. Even if they say the same thing as the teacher, often the comment has more weight coming from a peer.

Teachers should of course monitor feedback, as some students will need guidance in constructive commenting. Asking students to focus feedback on the positive elements—that is, on what went well—often requires detailed listening.

When sharing musical selfies, students will see other musicians at varying levels and can be both teacher to the less experienced students and inspired by those more advanced. Sharing practice goals and challenges helps students remember that they are part of a larger musical community—that they aren't alone in their practicing.

Practice stories

Text-based social media allows students to tell the story of their daily practice by blogging or microblogging.[28] Depending on the platform (e.g., Facebook, blogs, Twitter, Snapchat), students can write short status updates or lengthy descriptions about their practice goals, accomplishments, successes, and challenges. Students can post how they felt about their practice (maybe even in the form of emojis or animated gifs), or crowdsource a solution to a musical problem. Students who gravitate toward journaling may find this activity particularly appealing.

Practice stories go beyond the musical selfies, requiring a deeper level of reflection. Of course, students can highlight their practice stories by attaching photos or videos—for instance, adding a photo of their hand position or markings in the musical score. Recordings don't need to be extensive; ten- to fifteen-second audio or video clips will often be sufficient.

Posing questions online to seek an answer from a group of people (i.e., crowdsourcing) is now common on various social media platforms such as blogs and Facebook. This can easily be applied to musical practice. The problem-solving relationship between teacher and student is broadened to include other members of the class or studio. Students must reflect on their practice to figure out what musical problems they are facing and form a specific question to ask their peers. Appropriate questions might include:

- Where's the best place to breathe in the passage at circle A?
- Is there an alternative bowing (fingering) for measure 3?
- What's your favorite recording of the Bach's *Well-Tempered Clavier*?

The variety of solutions suggested by peers expands the student's perspective on the problem. Students now come to their lessons armed with possible answers to challenges faced in their daily practice. Teachers can help students sift through the ideas to find one that might solve their particular musical problem.

Another way to approach practice stories is to ask students to post a teaching tip every week on social media. These will likely come out of their practicing experiences. This encourages students to think more deeply about what they have learned and organize their thoughts to present to a virtual audience. Some students really connect with the role of teacher and can produce entire teacher-tip vlogs.

Virtual practice partners

Earlier in this chapter, we presented the idea of practice partners—students who work together to make practicing a more social experience. Practice partners can be in the same room together or brought together by technology (e.g., Skype, Google Hangouts).[29] After using this technology frequently it seems to disappear, leaving only the interaction—as if the other person is in the same room. Students can perform for each other and talk about music and technique.

The technology is advanced enough that audio quality is rarely a problem, and Internet lag or delay is continually improving. These advances in technology make virtual practice partners much more viable.

Teachers might be surprised at how much students working together can accomplish. When composer and researcher Lucy Green asked middle-school students to learn a piece of popular music without teacher intervention, they were surprisingly self-teaching.[30] The students working as a group provided motivation to practice, and ultimately helped make the students better musicians.

Musical practice can be a social activity with the use of technology, alleviating the normal isolation that comes with daily practice. Today's students use social media as part of their lives to connect with others. These same platforms allow students to share their musical journeys and learn from each other. Whichever platform is used, encourage students to be creative. The more creative the students are, the more interaction they will have, and the more motivated they will be to practice—and that's what it's all about!

Skyping together

Music teachers can integrate distance education into their studios or classes to varying degrees. Some exclusively teach online, using programs like Skype, but others use the technology more strategically.[31] Snow days no longer have to mean rescheduling lessons.

For applied teachers, online lessons can offer flexibility in certain situations. For instance, inclement weather would normally lead to lesson cancellations. With Skype or Google Hangouts, students can keep their lesson time—at home instead. No need to cancel and reschedule lessons! Students and teachers can connect using their mobile devices. Online lessons are also handy when the teacher has unexpected or frequent travel. Lessons can still be taught from a temporary studio or even a hotel room, in a pinch.

Another reason to offer lessons at a distance is to teach students who are geographically isolated from a quality music teacher (i.e., the teacher or students live in rural environments). Online lessons are also a possibility when a student moves, but is very attached to his or her teacher. Parents may not wish to give up a good relationship to find a new music instructor. In these cases, online teaching is limited to just a few students for specific reasons. In other words, the entire music studio does not necessarily need to be taught at a distance.

Online lessons can also supplement face-to-face lessons. Scheduling short five- to ten-minute midweek check-ups with students using Skype or FaceTime allows teachers to make adjustments earlier in the learning process. These scheduled mini-lessons can motivate students to practice and provide a level of supervision, which generally leads to more effective practice.[32] Teachers can include the mini-lesson option as part of a total private lesson package, but this could also be presented to parents as an optional extra, much like tutoring would be for academic subjects. These online mini-lessons may also be perfect over holiday breaks or vacations, when good intentions to practice are sometimes forgotten amidst life's distractions.

Other observers or active participants can also Skype into the lesson. This means that parents can be involved in the music lesson even if they are at work or traveling.

BOX 5.3 Visit the companion website

See companion website 5.2 for an example of a virtual master class given by book author Barbara Fast.

Distance education also opens up the option of having multiple teachers teaching as a team. This could include specialty teachers, brought in for a lesson or two to solve a specific technical problem or to cover a particular topic (e.g., improvisation), or who are familiar with a unique repertoire selection or composer. Finally, other students can observe lessons or participate in partner lessons from a distance. This can be particularly beneficial if students are studying, or about to study, the same repertoire. Partner lessons can be conducted in person, but scheduling partner lessons is simplified by the technology.

Extending the idea of teaching lessons online is the virtual master class, where a guest performer provides feedback to student musicians from a distance. Both studio and classroom teachers of all levels can arrange for a virtual master class. Master teachers from all over the world are now more easily accessible via the web, and virtual master classes are becoming more common at the university level.[33] There has even been exploration of collaborative playing at a distance, where performers interact in real time.

It's surprising how fast we can adapt to interacting online. At first, the interaction may feel awkward in comparison to in-person lessons, but once the music takes over the technology disappears into the background. One research study by Evelyn Orman and Jennifer Whitaker even found performance benefits for teaching applied lessons online versus face-to-face.[34] Many people use apps such as Skype for daily interactions, even preferring them to phone conversations.

Conclusion

Musical practice has traditionally been an isolated activity, but 21st-century technology allows musicians to connect and share with each other. Music teaching can now move beyond the four walls of a studio or classroom, taking advantage of online learning and social media—in essence, creating a virtual studio space.

Motivation to practice is the goal, whether using scoring systems that turn practice into a game or leveraging social media to share musical successes and challenges with peers.

Social media can be a powerful tool for good music. Used with innovation, social media can change the way we interact with our students and how they musically interact with each other.

Notes

1. Reed Larson explores how people feel when alone in his research study "The Solitary Side of Life."
2. Reed Larson and Mihaly Csikszentmihalyi report on how adolescents feel about being alone in their article "The Significance of Time Alone in Adolescent Development."
3. For a scholarly yet readable text exploring Vygotsky's theories see Yurly Karpov's book *Vygotsky for Educators*. Jackie Wiggins's book *Teaching for Musical Understanding* applies the theories of Vygotsky to the music classroom.
4. Information about the digital activity tracker Toggl may be found at https://toggl.com, and ATracker at www.wonderapps.se/atracker. The ProMusical music practice app may be found at https://itunes.apple.com/us/app/promusica-music-practice-journal-issue-tracker-metronome/id1037135905?mt=8.
5. MyFitnessPal is a nutrition and exercise tracker that includes musical performance as an exercise activity. Information may be found at www.myfitnesspal.com. Estimates of how many calories are used when practicing vary by instrument and body weight (and probably by repertoire). There is research behind some of these numbers, including a study by Claudia Iñesta and colleagues, "Heart Rate in Professional Musicians."
6. Susan Hallam wrote a comprehensive article titled "Musical Motivation" outlining research on practice motivation.
7. In general, research shows that students do not practice as much as a teacher expects during the week. One such paper on the topic was written by Marilyn J. Kostka, titled "Practice Expectations and Attitudes."
8. TripAdvisor is an online travel review website found at www.tripadvisor.com. They have a well-developed system for keeping reviewers motivated and submitting thoughts on restaurants, hotels, and other travel-related activities.
9. More information about the Pomodoro technique may be found in Francesco Cirillo's book *The Pomodoro Technique*.
10. The Tomato One time management app may be found at https://itunes.apple.com/us/app/tomato-one-free-focus-timer/id907364780?mt=12.
11. Decide Now!, a randomizer app, may be found at https://itunes.apple.com/us/app/decide-now/id383718755?mt=8.
12. For instance, John Geringer and Marilyn J. Kostka asked college students to describe what they did in the practice room, both performance and nonperformance activities, and compared the reports with actual practice room behaviors. These students performed a lot less than they thought and did twice as many nonperformance activities. See their study "An Analysis of Practice Room Behavior of College Music Students."
13. In one study, ice skaters reported that their goal was to practice difficult jumps more, but when practice was observed, the skaters practiced easier jumps more often—without realizing it. This finding was reported by J. M. Deakin and Stephen Cobley in the chapter "An Examination of the Practice Environments in Figure Skating and Volleyball" in Janet Starkes and K. Anders Ericsson's book *Expert Performance in Sports*.
14. Robert Duke and colleagues have researched the effects of sleep on successful musical performance. Practice followed by periods of sleep allows information to be consolidated and the material is better retained. See their article "Effects of Sleep on Performance of a Keyboard Melody" as an example.
15. Information about the app Interval Timer may be found at www.intervaltimer.com/create/hiit-timer.
16. The ProMusica app may be found at https://itunes.apple.com/us/app/promusica-music-practice-journal-issue-tracker-metronome/id1037135905?mt=8.
17. We thank band director Donna Schwartz for introducing us to the idea of the Rule of 10s in her August 20, 2015 blog posting found at https://donnaschwartzmusic.com/practice-rule-of-10s.
18. Collabra is a subscription-based service that hosts hours of practice recordings. More information may be found at https://wordpress.collabramusic.com. Information about iScore, a practice and communication tool, may be found at https://musictoolsuite.ca/iscore.

19. Burst mode was inspired by a blog posting about how to use timers in the practice room, written by guitar instructor Allen Mathews, that may be found at www.classicalguitarshed.com/timer.
20. There are many counting apps. Bean Count https://itunes.apple.com/us/app/bean-a-counting-app/id551418848?mt=8 and Counter—Tally Counter https://itunes.apple.com/us/app/counter-tally-counter/id1144352844?mt=8 are just two examples.
21. Go to the following websites for more information about the list-making apps Trello https://trello.com and Productive http://productiveapp.io.
22. For more information about practically gamifying everyday aspects of life see Brian Burke's book *Gamify*. For a research perspective on gamifying learning, see the chapter "Studying Gamification: The Effect of Rewards and Incentives on Motivation" by Ganit Richter, Daphne R. Raban, and Sheizaf Rafaeli, published in the book *Gamification in Education and Business*.
23. Information about Toodledo may be found at www.toodledo.com.
24. Information about Practice Buddy may be found at www.practicebuddyapp.com.
25. Go to https://jeopardylabs.com/build to start building a free online Jeopardy game.
26. Get started with Habitica by visiting their webpage at https://habitica.com.
27. At the time of writing, Facebook (www.facebook.com) was the most actively used social media platform with nearly 2 billion users. Instagram (www.instagram.com) is a popular photo-sharing space, but at the time of writing also allowed sixty-second videos to be shared, which is more than enough to give a picture of practicing. YouTube (www.youtube.com) is a popular video-sharing site. Prerecorded videos may be uploaded, but there is also a live-streaming feature. In Snapchat (www.snapchat.com), photos and videos disappear after they are shared. In May 2017, Snapchat introduced "custom stories," letting users collaboratively make stories combining their captures. Writing about practice within the 140-character limit of Twitter (https://twitter.com) means the students really have to think about what's important about their practicing.
28. Micro-blogging is shorter and simpler form of blogging, using shortened sentences that are more like an instant message, status updates, and images.
29. Skype (www.skype.com) and Google Hangouts (https://hangouts.google.com) are similar in that users interact in real time in a video version of a phone call. In fact, this entire book was written using Skype and Google Docs (www.google.com/docs/about), a program that let us edit the text of this book from a distance in real time. Skype and Google Docs allowed us to work as if we were in the same room rather than in separate states.
30. Lucy Green describes a project where middle-school students learned popular music in a social group in the article "The Music Curriculum as Lived Experience."
31. To see an example of group and private lessons taught online, see pianist Bradley Sowash's website, especially his video on how to setup the online lessons, at https://bradleysowash.com/group-lessons.
32. Musician Nancy Barry and music psychologist Susan Hallam wrote a comprehensive and easy to understand overview of musical practice from a research perspective including the positive influences of supervision in the chapter "Practice" in Richard Parncutt and Gary McPherson's book *The Science and Psychology of Music Performance*.
33. For an example of a virtual master class, see Anne Epperson at www.youtube.com/watch?v=FJNFuY-glxg.
34. Evelyn K. Orman and Jennifer A. Whitaker compared nonverbal communication in face-to-face lessons and videoconference lessons with the same students. Both performance and eye contact increased during the videoconference lessons. Their results are published in the article "Time Usage During Face-to-Face and Synchronous Distance Music Lessons."

Coda

This book has been first and foremost about practicing strategies that integrate current, easy-to-use technology. The goal of this book is to help students become better musicians—period. Rather than replacing quality practice strategies, technology brings new tools to the practicing toolbox. New practice strategies emerge with new technology.

Some strategies in this book would not have been possible without advances in technology; others expand tried-and-true practice strategies with the use of technology. We've made a concerted effort to future-proof this book by focusing on music practice strategies rather than the specific technology, since technology continues to evolve—seemingly at the speed of light.

As technology improves, ironically, it begins to disappear into the background, becoming transparent. Better technology simply gets out of the way of the music. Teachers don't have to teach to the technology. Music and music learning remain the focus. There may be a learning curve when using some of the technologies presented in this book, but they are well within reach of anyone who has figured out how to work their iPhone. Most students will be able to pick up and use these technologies quickly and easily.

Some of the practice strategies presented in this book change the relationship between teacher and student and question assumptions about how we have traditionally learned musical skills. Flipping the classroom and hybrid performances are cases in point. The technology empowers student learning and the teacher may become more of a facilitator—a role that is much more fun! This creates an independent learning environment. These strategies help us think creatively about what we do in music lessons and how we interact with students.

All the technologies included in this book are widely accessible. Most are free or inexpensive, and don't require extensive specialist equipment or learning. We've focused on everyday technology and on how this technology can be repurposed for musical practice. We have not included advanced technology that requires intensive training or expensive hardware or software. For instance, we have not discussed virtual acoustic environments, stand-alone practice rooms that will simulate the acoustics of various concert halls. These may help students prepare for performance, but are generally beyond the means of the average musician.[1]

Technology has changed so many aspects of our lives, and now it's expanding our practice possibilities. Tomorrow, a new technology will emerge that can be repurposed for musical practice. The hope is that in reading this book, teachers think creatively about music teaching and will quickly see how this emerging technology can be integrated into their lessons. For instance, voice-command technologies (e.g., Siri, Echo) and VR (virtual reality) are becoming very common. The question is: How can these be used in the music studio to advance musical learning?

Look closely at the technologies we use every day and see the possibilities . . .

Note

1. For more information on virtual acoustic environments, see www.wengercorp.com/sound-isolation/virtual-acoustic-environment-technology.php.

Bibliography

Alexander, Dennis, Gayle Kowalchyk, E. L. Lancaster, Victoria McArthur, and Martha Mier. *Alfred's Premier Piano Course Technique 2B*. Van Nuys, CA: Alfred Publishing, 2006.

Barbuscia, Aurelie. "Musical Practice Halfway between Art and Mechanics: The Effects of the Metronome on the Musical World in the 19th Century." *Revue d'Histoire du XIX Siecle* 45 (2012): 236.

Barry, Nancy. "A Qualitative Study of Applied Music Lessons and Subsequent Student Practice Sessions." *Contributions to Music Education* 34 (2007): 51–65.

Barry, Nancy, and Victoria McArthur. "Teaching Practice Strategies in the Music Studio: A Survey of Applied Music Teachers." *Psychology of Music* 22 (1994): 44–55.

Baumeister, Roy F., Ellen Bratslavsky, Catrin Finkenauer, and Kathleen D. Vohs. "Bad Is Stronger than Good." *Review of General Psychology* 5 (2001): 323–370.

Breth, Nancy. *Practicing the Piano—How Students Parents & Teachers Can Make Practicing More Effective*. Milwaukee, WI: Hal Leonard, 2012.

Brown, Peter, Henry Roediger, and Mark McDaniel. *Make It Stick: The Science of Successful Learning*. Cambridge, MA: The Belknap Press of Harvard University Press, 2014.

Bruser, Madeline. *The Art of Practicing*. New York: Three Rivers Press, 1997.

Bugos, Jennifer, and Linda High. "Perceived Versus Actual Practice Strategy Usage by Older Adult Novice Piano Students." *Visions of Research in Music Education* 13 (2009). www-usr.rider.edu/~vrme/v13n1/Vision/Bugos.%20Final%20ed%20fa.01.14.09.pdf.

Burke, Brian. *Gamify: How Gamification Motivates People to Do Extraordinary Things*. New York: Routledge, 2016.

Carey, Benedict. *How We Learn: The Surprising Truth About When, Where, and Why It Happens*. New York: Random House, 2015.

Carter, Christine, and Jessica Grahn. "Optimizing Music Learning: Exploring How Blocked and Interleaved Practice Schedules Affect Advanced Performance." *Frontiers in Psychology* 7 (2016): 1251. www.frontiersin.org/articles/10.3389/fpsyg.2016.01251/full.

Chaffin, Roger. "Learning *Clair de Lune*: Retrieval Practice and Expert Memorization." *Music Perception* 24 (2007): 377–393.

Chaffin, Roger, and Gabriela Imreh. "Pulling Teeth and Torture: Musical Memory and Problem Solving." *Thinking and Reasoning* 3 (1997): 315–336.

Chaffin, Roger, Gabriela Imreh, and Mary Crawford. *Practicing Perfection: Memory and Piano Performance*. New York: Psychology Press, 2002.

Chase, William, and Hebert Simon. "Perception in Chess." *Cognitive Psychology* 4 (1973): 55–81.

Cirillo, Francesco. *The Pomodoro Technique: The Acclaimed Time Management System That Has Transformed How We Work*. London: Ebury Publishing, 2018.

Deakin, Janice. *Expert Performance in Sports: Advances in Research on Sport Expertise*. Champaign, IL: Human Kinetics, 2003.

Duke, Robert, and Amy Simmons. "Effects of Sleep on Performance of a Keyboard Melody." *Journal of Research in Music Education* 54 (2006): 257–269.

Duncker, Karl. "On Problem-Solving." *Psychological Monographs* 58, no. 5 (1945): i–113.

Ericsson, Anders, Ralf Krampe, and Clemens Tesch-Romer. "The Role of Deliberate Practice in the Acquisition of Expert Performance." *Psychological Review* 100, no. 3 (1993): 363–406.

Foer, Joshua. *Moonwalking with Einstein: The Art and Science of Remembering Everything*. London: Penguin, 2011.

Forscher, Susan, Russell E. Murray, and Cynthia J. Cyrus. *Music Education in the Middle Ages and the Renaissance*. Bloomington: Indiana University Press, 2010.

Geringer, John, and Marilyn J. Kostka. "An Analysis of Practice Room Behavior of College Music Students." *Contributions to Music Education* 11 (1984): 24–27.

Gladwell, Malcolm. *Outliers*. Boston: Little, Brown, 2008.

Green, Lucy. "The Music Curriculum as Lived Experience: Children's 'Natural' Music-Learning Processes." *Music Educators Journal* 91 (2005): 27–32.

Hallam, Susan. "Musical Motivation: Towards a Model Synthesising the Research." *Music Education Research* 4 (2002): 225–244.

Hallam, Susan, Ian Cross, and Michael H. Thaut. *Oxford Handbook of Music Psychology*. New York: Oxford University Press, 2016.

Hewitt, Michael P. "The Effects of Modeling, Self-Evaluation, and Self-Listening on Junior High Instrumentals' Music Performance and Practice Attitude." *Journal of Research in Music Education* 49 (2016): 307–322.

Iñesta, Claudia, Nicolás Terrados, Daniel García, and José A. Pérez. "Heart Rate in Professional Musicians." *Journal of Occupational Medicine and Toxicology* 3, no. 16 (2008): 1–11.

Johnson, Phillip. *The Practice Revolution: Getting Great Results from the Six Days Between Lessons*. Pearce, Australia: PracticeSpot Press, 2006.

Jørgensen, Harald. "Strategies for Individual Practice." In *Musical Excellence: Strategies and Techniques to Enhance Performance*, edited by Aaron Williamon, 85–104. Oxford: Oxford University Press, 2011.

Karageorghis, Costas I., and Terry Peter. *Inside Sport Psychology*. Champaign, IL: Human Kinetics, 2011.

Karpov, Yurly. *Vygotsky for Educators*. New York: Cambridge University Press, 2014.

Katz, Mark. *Capturing Sound: How Technology Has Changed Music*. Berkeley: University of California Press, 2004.

Kearns, Ronald E. *Recording Tips for Music Education: A Practical Guide for Recording School Groups*. New York: Oxford University Press, 2017.

Kelly, Thomas Forrest. *Capturing Music: The Story of Notation*. New York: Norton, 2015.

Kenny, Dianna. *The Psychology of Music Performance Anxiety*. Oxford: Oxford University Press, 2011.

Klickstein, Gerald. *The Musician's Way*. Oxford: Oxford University Press, 2009.

Kostka, Marilyn J. "Practice Expectations and Attitudes: A Survey of College-Level Music Teachers and Students." *Journal of Research in Music Education* 50, no. 2 (2002): 145–154.

Kozulin, Alex. *Vygotsky's Educational Theory in Cultural Context*. Cambridge: Cambridge University Press, 2007.

Larson, Reed. "The Solitary Side of Life: An Examination of the Time People Spend Alone from Childhood to Old Age." *Developmental Review* 10 (1990):155–183.

Larson, Reed, and Mihaly Csikszentmihalyi. "The Significance of Time Alone in Adolescent Development." *Journal of Current Adolescent Medicine* 2 (1980): 33–40.

Levitin, Daniel. *This Is Your Brain on Music*. New York: Dutton, 2016.

Manfredo, Joseph. "Effective Time Management in Ensemble Rehearsals." *Music Educator's Journal* 93 (2006): 42–46.

Meyer, Frederic Charles. *New Treatise on the Art of Playing upon the Double Movement Harp, Comprising the Rudiments of Music a Series of Exercises in which is Shown a Mode of Advantageously Employing the Metronome and a Concise Theory upon Practical Harmony*. London: J. Green, circa 1825.

Mishra, Jennifer. "Improving Sightreading Accuracy: A Meta-Analysis." *Psychology of Music* 42, no. 2 (2014): 131–156.

Mishra, Jennifer. "Musical Expertise." In *The Oxford Handbook of Expertise: Research & Application*, edited by Paul Ward, Jan Maarten Schraagen, Julie Gore, and Emilie Roth. New York: Oxford University Press, in press.

Mishra, Jennifer, and Barbara Fast. "Practising in the New World: A Case Study of Practising Strategies Related to the Premiere of Contemporary Music." *Music Performance Research* 7 (2015): 65–80. www.mpr-online.net/Issues/Volume%207%20[2015]/MPR0102%20Mishra%20and%20Fast%20(2015).pdf.

O'Brien, Orin. *Double Bass Notebook*. New York: Carl Fischer, 2016.

Odam, George. *The Sounding Symbol: Music Education in Action*. Cheltenham: Stanley Thornes, 1995.

Oh, Eunjung, and Thomas C. Reeves. "Generational Differences and the Integration of Technology in Learning, Instruction, and Performance." In *Handbook of Research on Educational Communications and Technology*, edited by J. Michael Spector, 819–828. New York: Springer, 2014.

Orman, Evelyn K., and Jennifer A. Whitaker. "Time Usage During Face-to-Face and Synchronous Distance Music Lessons." *American Journal of Distance Education* 24 (2010): 92–103.

Parncutt, Richard, and Gary McPherson. *The Science and Psychology of Music Performance: Creative Strategies for Teaching and Learning*. Oxford: Oxford University Press, 2002.

Pearce, Elvina. *The Success Factor in Piano Teaching: Making Practice Perfect*. Kingston, New Jersey: The Frances Clark Center for Keyboard Pedagogy, Inc., 2014.

Pike, Pamela, and Rebecca Carter. "Employing Cognitive Chunking Techniques to Enhance Sight-Reading Performance of Undergraduate Group-Piano Students." *International Journal of Music Education* 28 (2010): 231–246.

Poli, Roberto. *The Secret Life of Musical Notation: Defying Interpretive Traditions*. Milwaukee, WI: Amadeus, 2010.

Richter, Ganit, Daphne R. Raban, Sheizaf and Rafaeli. *Gamification in Education and Business*. Cham, Switzerland: Springer International Publishing, 2015.

Rohwer, Debbie, and Jeremy Polk. "Practice Behaviors of 8th Grade Instrumental Musicians." *Journal of Research in Music Education* 54 (2006): 350–362.

Shockley, Rebecca Payne. *Mapping Music: For Faster Learning and Secure Memory*. Middleton, WI: A-R Editions, 2001.

Simmons, Amy. "Distributed Practice and Procedural Memory Consolidation in Musicians' Skill Learning." *Journal of Research in Music Education* 59 (2012): 357–368.

Sloboda, John. "The Effect of Item Position on the Likelihood of Identification by Inference in Prose Reading and Music Reading." *Canadian Journal of Psychology* 30 (1976): 228–237.

Sloboda, John. "The Uses of Space in Music Notation." *Visible Language* 15 (1981): 86–110.

Spector, J. Michael. *Handbook of Research on Educational Communications and Technology*. New York: Springer, 2014.

Stambaugh, Laura. "When Repetition Isn't the Best Practice Strategy: Effects of Blocked and Random Practice Schedules." *Journal of Research in Music Education* 54 (2011): 368–383.

Starkes, Janet L., and K. Anders Ericsson. *Expert Performance in Sports: Advances in Research on Sport Expertise*. Champaign, IL: Human Kinetics, 2003.

Suzuki, Shinichi. *Nurtured By Love: The Classic Approach to Talent Education*. Princeton, NJ: Summy-Birchard, 1995.

Tucker, Bill. "The Flipped Classroom: Online Instruction at Home Frees Class Time for Learning." *Education Next* (2012). https://docs.google.com/viewer?a=vandpid=sitesandsrcid=ZGVmYXVsdGRvbWFpbnxramFtYXRoNTM1fGd4OmRkNGYwMDI5YmEyYjhjNw.

Ward, Paul, Jan Maarten Schraagen, Julie Gore, and Emilie Roth. *The Oxford Handbook of Expertise: Research and Application*. New York: Oxford University Press, in press.

Weekley, Dallas, and Nancy Arganbright. *The Piano Duet: A Learning Guide*. San Diego, CA: Neil A. Kjos, 1996.

Wesolowski, Brian C. "Understanding and Developing Rubrics for Music Performance Assessment." *Music Educator's Journal* 98 (2012): 36–42.

Wiggins, Jackie. *Teaching for Musical Understanding*. New York: McGraw-Hill, 2001.

Williamon, Aaron. *Musical Excellence: Strategies and Techniques to Enhance Performance*. Oxford: Oxford University Press, 2011.

Williamon, Aaron, and Elizabeth Valentine. "The Role of Retrieval Structures in Memorizing Music." *Cognitive Psychology* 44 (2002): 1–32.

Index

www.ingramcontent.com/pod-product-compliance
Ingram Content Group UK Ltd.
Pitfield, Milton Keynes, MK11 3LW, UK
UKHW051130260726
13967UKWH00010B/2956

9 780190 660901